Lita Linzer Schwartz, PhD

I0628346

When Adoptions
Go Wrong
Psychological and Legal Issues

Pre-publication
REVIEWS,
COMMENTARIES,
EVALUATIONS . . .

"The problem of adoption disruption is very real. The media emphasizes the traumatic public cases, but hundreds more occur yearly without media fanfare. The risks of disruption to adoptive families—and to children—are too often downplayed by even well-meaning agencies, attorneys, and social workers. This book is a thoughtful analysis of a too-often neglected issue. The focus on the child's best interest is hopeful and refreshing. As an attorney who has handled many successful adoptions, and a few heartbreaking adoption disruptions, I greatly admire Dr. Schwartz's humanistic view of this troubling issue."

Dana Rakinic, JD
Parnter, Rakinic & Mezzy LLC

"The author does an excellent job of taking the reader through an understanding of the psychological and legal complexities of adoption, providing a compelling description of the difficulties being faced by both children and adults when there is a disruption of an adoption. In a very readable book, Dr. Linzer Schwartz provides sound recommendations to help fix a very broken system. More than anything, her unyielding demand for the system to place the highest emphasis on children's rights and needs is refreshing. I would urge all judges, children's rights attorneys, lobbyists for children, social workers, and other mental help professionals who work with adopting families to read this book and advocate for the children who are most affected when adoptions get disrupted."

Philip M. Stahl, PhD
CA Licensed Psychologist
in Private Practice,
West Palm Beach, Florida

More pre-publication
REVIEWS, COMMENTARIES, EVALUATIONS . . .

"**W***hen Adoptions Go Wrong: Psychological and Legal Issues of Adoption Disruption* is an informative book regarding the very complicated legal and emotional processes surrounding adoption from the start of the process through its possible disruption and dissolution."

Dr. Judith L. Newman, PhD
Associate Professor of Human Development and Family Studies, Penn State Abington

The Haworth Press
New York • London • Oxford

NOTES FOR PROFESSIONAL LIBRARIANS AND LIBRARY USERS

This is an original book title published by The Haworth Press, Inc. Unless otherwise noted in specific chapters with attribution, materials in this book have not been previously published elsewhere in any format or language.

CONSERVATION AND PRESERVATION NOTES

All books published by The Haworth Press, Inc., and its imprints are printed on certified pH neutral, acid-free book grade paper. This paper meets the minimum requirements of American National Standard for Information Sciences-Permanence of Paper for Printed Material, ANSI Z39.48-1984.

DIGITAL OBJECT IDENTIFIER (DOI) LINKING

The Haworth Press is participating in reference linking for elements of our original books. (For more information on reference linking initiatives, please consult the CrossRef Web site at www.crossref.org.) When citing an element of this book such as a chapter, include the element's Digital Object Identifier (DOI) as the last item of the reference. A Digital Object Identifier is a persistent, authoritative, and unique identifier that a publisher assigns to each element of a book. Because of its persistence, DOIs will enable The Haworth Press and other publishers to link to the element referenced, and the link will not break over time. This will be a great resource in scholarly research.

When Adoptions
Go Wrong
*Psychological and Legal Issues
of Adoption Disruption*

HAWORTH Marriage and Family Therapy
Terry S. Trepper, PhD
Senior Editor

When Adoptions Go Wrong
Psychological and Legal Issues of Adoption Disruption

Lita Linzer Schwartz, PhD

362.734
S399

The Haworth Press
New York • London • Oxford

LIBRARY
MILWAUKEE AREA TECHNICAL COLLEGE
Milwaukee Campus

For more information on this book or to order, visit
http://www.haworthpress.com/store/product.asp?sku=5780

or call 1-800-HAWORTH (800-429-6784) in the United States and Canada
or (607) 722-5857 outside the United States and Canada

or contact orders@HaworthPress.com

Published by

The Haworth Press, Inc., 10 Alice Street, Binghamton, NY 13904-1580.

© 2006 by The Haworth Press, Inc. All rights reserved. No part of this work may be reproduced or utilized in any form or by any means, electronic or mechanical, including photocopying, microfilm, and recording, or by any information storage and retrieval system, without permission in writing from the publisher. Printed in the United States of America.

Excerpts from Resnik (1996) Seeking the Wisdom of Solomon: Defining the Rights of Fathers in Newborn Adoptions, *Seton Hall Legislative Journal, 20,* 363-431 reprinted with permission.

PUBLISHER'S NOTE
The development, preparation, and publication of this work has been undertaken with great care. However, the Publisher, employees, editors, and agents of The Haworth Press are not responsible for any errors contained herein or for consequences that may ensue from use of materials or information contained in this work. The Haworth Press is committed to the dissemination of ideas and information according to the highest standards of intellectual freedom and the free exchange of ideas. Statements made and opinions expressed in this publication do not necessarily reflect the views of the Publisher, Directors, management, or staff of The Haworth Press, Inc., or an endorsement by them.

Cover design by Jennifer M. Gaska.

Library of Congress Cataloging-in-Publication Data

Schwartz, Lita Linzer.
    When adoptions go wrong : psychological and legal issues of adoption disruption / Lita Linzer Schwartz.
        p. cm.
    Includes bibliographical references and index.
    ISBN-13: 978-0-7890-3181-5 (hard : alk. paper)
    ISBN-10: 0-7890-3181-7 (hard : alk. paper)
    ISBN-13: 978-0-7890-3182-2 (soft : alk. paper)
    ISBN-10: 0-7890-3182-5 (soft : alk. paper)
    1. Adoption—Psychological aspects. 2. Adoption—Law and legislation. I. Title.

HV875.S3683 2006
362.734—dc22
                                                                                2006006907

With loving thanks for making us a family:

Arthur Lee

Joshua David

Frederic Seth

ABOUT THE AUTHOR

Lita Linzer Schwartz, PhD, is Distinguished Professor Emerita from Penn State, where she taught for many years at what is now Abington College of Penn State, near Philadelphia. She has been trained in family mediation, holds a Diplomate in Forensic Psychology, and is a Fellow of the American Psychological Association. Dr. Schwartz is co-author of several books and co-editor of *Welcome Home! An International and Nontraditional Adoption Reader* (Haworth). She began writing about adoption disputes more than twenty years ago and has had her work published in the *American Journal of Family Therapy, Family and Conciliation Courts Review,* the *Journal of Family Psychology,* and *Behavioral Sciences and the Law.* In recent years, she has emphasized the legal and psychological ramifications of child custody contests arising from adoption or divorce.

CONTENTS

Foreword

Because adoption has undergone dramatic changes during the past twenty years, there is a need for study and analysis of current trends. Dr. Lita Schwartz, a recognized expert in the field, has investigated the ways in which the changes have impacted on the ability to affect a smooth transfer of children to new homes and parents. A major area of concern is the rise in interrupted adoptions to an extent not envisioned in the mid-twentieth century.

During the post–World War II period adoptions were usually arranged between a husband and wife unable to bear children and a young mother who could not continue to support a child, whether due to community stigma or lack of economic prospects. Interrupted adoptions were rare, usually only occurring because the mother changed her mind and not because of other forces that are present today.

Today, a single woman bearing a child no longer has the stigma prevalent during the past century. Single-woman households are now quite common and are accepted by society. Also, a sea change has occurred in the pool of potential adopters. We have single women, single men, gay and lesbian couples, unmarried men and women living together, as well as married couples unable to bear children and not suitable for artificial insemination who seek to adopt children.

The changed profiles of the adoptive parents, combined with new reasons for wanting to adopt, have resulted in many more disrupted adoptions. The child's natural father may now appear on the scene as well as grandparents and other relatives of the natural mother. Concern arises that one or both of the natural parents may be seeking monetary gain by withholding or negating consent.

Dr. Schwartz's study delves into many reasons for the increase in disrupted adoptions. She has also included the latest legislation pertaining to adoption by gay couples and provides details of court cases in which reporters for the twenty-four-hour news media have become

When Adoptions Go Wrong
© 2006 by The Haworth Press, Inc. All rights reserved.
doi:10.1300/5780_a

involved by focusing on dramatic confrontations, making for good television ratings, but bad child rearing.

During the years I served as a judge in the Matrimonial Part of New York State Supreme Court, I saw, firsthand, the disruption caused in the lives of children faced with uncertainty regarding who would be their parents. As Dr. Schwartz has emphasized, that uncertainty can result in lasting damage to the children and adults directly involved as well as to other family members.

She properly blames the courts for seemingly unnecessary delays that make bad situations even worse and also highlights a lack of mental health services to aid the parties when an adoption goes awry. Her positive suggestions would enable professionals to ease the strain on children and parents, both natural and adoptive, and come at a time when the problems in the field must be addressed. Dr. Schwartz suggests legislative measures to create uniformity in the way states handle the issues that arise and deal with them more rapidly, thereby aiding the natural and adoptive parents in making difficult decisions. This valuable study should be essential reading for those in all fields related to adoption.

Hon. Walter M. Schackman
Justice of the Supreme Court
of the State of New York (retired)

Acknowledgments

This book grew from a workshop I was invited to present at the 11th National Conference on Children and the Law: Lawyers and Psychologists Working Together, cosponsored by the American Psychological Association and the American Bar Association, June 3-5, 2004, in Washington, DC. I am grateful to have had that opportunity to learn more about an area of children's lives that has been largely overlooked except in occasional headline stories.

Much of the research for the workshop and this book could not have been accomplished without the help of the Penn State Abington College Library staff, especially Jeannette Ullrich and Binh Le. They were always available to help with perplexing problems, for which I thank them profusely.

When Adoptions Go Wrong
© 2006 by The Haworth Press, Inc. All rights reserved.
doi:10.1300/5780_b

SECTION I:
FAMILY PSYCHOLOGY ISSUES

Chapter 1

Overview: Providing a Context

HISTORICAL BACKGROUND

Adoption as we know it early in the twenty-first century is a relatively modern phenomenon. The first comprehensive American law regarding adoption was passed in Massachusetts in 1851 (Spofford, 1993). It provided for written consent by the child's natural parent or legal guardian for the adoption, for the signature of the marital partner of the adopter on the adoption petition, and for the satisfaction of the probate judge to whom the petition was submitted that the prospective adoptive parents had the ability to rear the child satisfactorily. According to *The CQ Researcher* (Adoption, 1993), this was followed in 1881 by a Michigan law requiring judges to investigate would-be adoptive parents before issuing adoption decrees. Adoption in the nineteenth century, apart from conferring legal heir status on these children, also was an attempt to remove children from foundling homes, orphanages, and indentured service. These motives have continued to underlie adoption placements to the present day, though in perhaps more contemporary settings.

Adoption increased after World War I (and later WW II) to accommodate the needs of thousands of children left homeless in the aftermath of war. The U. S. Supreme Court ruled, in 1923 in the case of *Meyer v. Nebraska,* that the Fourteenth Amendment protects a parent's right to bring up children, somewhat maintaining the view of children as one's property. In 1972, in *Stanley v. Illinois,* the Court recognized the rights of unwed fathers in adoption proceedings for the first time. Less than a decade later, in 1983 in *Lehr v. Robinson,* however, the Court modified its earlier ruling by stating that a father who had never established a relationship with his child was not entitled to a notice of adoption[1] (Resnik, 1996).

When Adoptions Go Wrong
© 2006 by The Haworth Press, Inc. All rights reserved.
doi:10.1300/5780_01

3

In this same period, Congress passed the Indian Child Welfare Act in 1978, giving first preference to Native American families and tribes in the adoption of Indian children. At the core of this Act "was the question of tribal rights to direct the care and custody of children; by extension, it recognized the transmission of Indian culture to future generations" (Holt, 2001, p. 6). For decades, non-Indian social workers and others had removed Indian children from their tribal caretakers for a variety of reasons that reflected differing perspectives on child rearing, with the result that tens of thousands of these children had been placed in orphanages or foster care. In 1980, the Adoption Assistance and Child Welfare Act was passed, which provided funds to aid in finding permanent homes for special needs and other hard-to-place children who were in foster care.

Legislation passed in the first few decades of the twentieth century mandated secrecy, anonymity, and sealing of adoption records to shield these data and proceedings from public scrutiny. This was partly to protect the children from the stigma of illegitimacy and partly to protect the birth mothers' anonymity as childless couples began increasingly to adopt children. The adoptions by childless couples, and in some cases by couples with biological children, increased rapidly in the second half of the century to the point where there were not enough healthy children to meet the "demand" (Spofford, 1993). At the same time, international adoption became feasible, notably beginning with Pearl Buck's efforts on behalf of Chinese children in the 1930s and expanding to tens of thousands of children being adopted annually from all over the world by 2005.

The 1990s also brought protracted adoption battles for Babies Jessica, Richard, Emily, and others, as well as continuing conflict over the rights of homosexuals to adopt children. (The latter will be more formally discussed with reference to the *Lofton v. Kearney* case.) The Supreme Court's unwillingness to hear the Baby Richard and Baby Jessica cases "left the states wide latitude in crafting solutions to the dilemma posed by unwed fathers and newborn adoptions" (Resnik, 1996, p. 390). The result of that latitude has been considerable divergence among the states in perceptions of what constitutes appropriate support during pregnancy and postpregnancy for the mother to be, what efforts demonstrate the establishment of a parent-child relationship, how much time the unwed or putative father has to file his claim to paternity/opposition to adoption, and other related matters. The divergence is reflected in the volume of articles and books published in the mid-1990s and since with respect to these conflicted cases.

Mason (1994) has concluded that "the legal history of child custody is far more about the rights of mothers, fathers, and masters than it is about the welfare of children" (p. 188). Even at the end of the twentieth century, when Mason wrote, and early into the twenty-first century, it is evident that children, "who have no political voice, are too often the political weapons of others' battles or, simply, are not considered at all" (p. 189). (This has also long been this author's position with respect to children caught in divorce or adoption custody conflicts.) The lack of a voice in court as well, contributes too often to the negative consequences of custody disputes for children's "best interests."

MALFUNCTIONS IN ADOPTION

Technically, "adoption disruption" describes the ending of an adoption process when the adoption has not yet been legally finalized, while "adoption dissolution" describes the end of an adoption that has already been finalized (Marian Adoption Services, 1999). In the latter situation, it may be that the adopting parents cannot handle the child for some reason, or that the court has determined that there is a significant reason to vacate the adoption. Whichever of these events occurs, someone's parental rights must be terminated in court. As a practical matter, however, all abrogations of an adoption will here be considered "disruptions" since lives are being disrupted even as relationships are being dissolved.

A disrupted adoption can affect those immediately concerned in different ways and for differing periods of time, but may also affect other people in a ripple-type effect depending on their relationship to those intimately concerned, or the amount of publicity a particular case receives. Certainly the "Baby Jessica" and "Baby Richard" cases of the early 1990s (Meyer, 1999; Rosenman, 1995; Weaver-Catalana, 1995) created pangs in the hearts of hundreds of thousands of people who only knew of these cases through the news media. These two cases, among others, posed the crucial question of whether the babies were seen as people or possessions. In other cases as well,

> Compared with women with no fertility problems, . . . infertility
> is associated with substantial and significant long-term psycho-
> logical distress only for women with no children at all, social or
> biological. . . . The strong, long-term effect of motherhood de-
> nied supports an argument that frustrated attempts to achieve
> motherhood threaten a central life identity. (McQuillen, Greil,
> White, & Jacob, 2003, p. 1015)

By contrast, adoptive parenthood, according to couples in another
study, "helped to heal the hurt of being infertile" (Daniluk & Hurtig-
Mitchell, 2003, p. 396). They also felt that the effort it took to become
adoptive parents, as well as their commitment, made them better prepared to be caring, loving parents.

Those with fertility problems may also have to cope with the financial charges for treatment that may not be totally covered by an HMO
or other insurance carrier. These can range from $1,000 to $2,000 for
fertility pills or artificial insemination, and up to $20,000 to $35,000
for in vitro fertilization with donor eggs (Kolata, 2004). If the first attempt is unsuccessful, the costs and pain recur the next time around,
and the try after that. After one or two years of treatment, the couple
may say "enough!" and opt to adopt. Which path they take to adoption may vary with their preferences or limitations, their location, and
other factors. However, if they take the route to international adoption, as has been done more frequently in recent years, they will find
that the dollar cost of an overseas adoption is about that of an in vitro
insemination, but with somewhat better odds of having a child as a
result of the expenditure (Schwartz & Kaslow, 2003).

The problem of becoming a parent may not be infertility, but simply absence of a partner with whom to conceive and possibly raise a
child. Although adoption is more often the choice of single females,
more recently single men have also taken the adoption route to fulfill
their desire to become fathers (Mannis, 2000; Shireman, 1995). Surrogacy is another path that may be followed with the same outcome,
but many prospective parents have questions or reservations about
postnatal complications in the relationships and therefore prefer and
ultimately choose adoption (Schwartz, 1991). Similar problems may
occur for same-sex couples, who resort to alternative reproductive
technologies in order to have a child. Adoption becomes part of the
picture here because the partner wishes to become an adoptive parent

of the child and, in most cases, is not allowed to be so named because of state law[2] (Schwartz, 2003).

In some cases, adoptive parents may have been foster parents to a child and then chose to adopt him or her when the child became available for adoption. The continuing relationship is considered a positive resource with less likelihood for adoption disruption (Barth & Berry, 1988). Sometimes financial aid from the state is attached to the adoption, as in the case of a special needs child. This may or may not be an added factor in choosing to adopt the child.

Other potential parents may seek to give a child a better chance in life than repeated moves among foster homes or long stays in orphanages provide. Many of these people have decided, for a variety of reasons, to seek a child overseas where care tends to be very poor. A number of adoptive parents discussed almost all of these possibilities in *Welcome Home! An International and Nontraditional Adoption Reader* (Schwartz & Kaslow, 2003). In this book, one finds a strong sense of commitment, a definite intention to adopt—whatever the reason. They make it clear, moreover, that if there is a partner or a mate, the decision to adopt must be mutual.

If either partner has reservations about adoption, "the couple should postpone any such action until they can go forward in agreement and with a positive attitude, even if they have some natural anxieties about how the placement will work out" (Schwartz, 2000b, p. 268). Reluctance on the part of one partner will inevitably affect not only the parent-child relationship, but also the adult partnership. Disagreement on how to go about adopting or about the background of the child to be adopted can be worked out more easily than overcoming reluctance.

Types of Adoption

Traditional adoption includes:

Adoption agency
Independent adoption through an intermediary (e.g., doctor, lawyer)

Contemporary adoption includes:

Grandparent or skipped-generation adoption
Adoption from foster placement

Open adoption
Special needs adoption
Internet adoption
Overseas adoption
Transracial adoption
Adoption by homosexual/lesbian couples

As will be seen, the contemporary modes of adoption have become dominant in recent years, although most of them are still accomplished through use of one of the traditional means. Advantages and disadvantages, as well as why some of these modes are more likely to lead to disruption, should be considered by the prospective parent(s) as part of deciding "who" to adopt.

Who Shall I/We Adopt?

Having decided to adopt, the prospective parents must make a number of decisions about *who* to adopt. They need to consider age of the child, perhaps gender, religious concerns, racial or ethnic background, and whether the child has special needs due to physical or emotional conditions. If they have one or more children in the family already, they should consider the impact of adoption on them also. They should ask such children, if old enough to comprehend the question, how they feel about the possible adoption. The changes in the family due to the arrival of another child (whether by birth, foster care, or adoption), will, after all, affect them. With children old enough to understand, the parents should certainly stress the positive aspects of the changes, but also indicate their awareness that the child(ren) already present may feel more threatened to some degree than ecstatic. This, of course, varies with the child.

If the child available for adoption has special needs, a number of questions should be raised. Does the child have any sensory or mobility limitations? Are the prospective parents prepared to deal with medical and/or emotional problems? Do they have the financial resources or supplementary support sources to pay for therapy, whether medical and/or psychological? (Note: In some cases, they will receive financial aid from the state for assuming responsibility for the care of the special needs child.) Will they have physical and emotional support from extended family members and friends if they choose to parent a child with such problems?

Although children already in the family, by birth or adoption, should be included in the parents' decision to "expand" the family as already mentioned, this is even more important if the prospective sibling is a child with special needs. Ideally, the family would participate in an adoption education program that would prepare all members for the strengths and stresses involved in the new situation. If the children already present are not included in the preadoption process, they may be vulnerable to "sadness, anger, resentment, depression, withdrawal, acting out, and/or embarrassment" (Mullin & Johnson, 1999, p. 582). On the other hand, the parents should make clear that they are considering the children's opinions in deciding whether to adopt, but that (at least under most circumstances) those opinions, even or especially if negative, may not be determinative. It would seem wise, however, to explore why the children hold the negative opinions, and whether their reasons go beyond the somewhat normal anxiety of having competition for the parents' affection and attention. Barth and Brooks (1997) found that some tensions affected the interaction between biological and adopted children even in the absence of special needs.

Perhaps with the guidance of a supportive social worker, the parents can acknowledge that the arrival of another child, especially one with special needs, will bring changes to the family's life, *but*—to the child—"Here's how you can help." Even a two-year-old can fetch a diaper, a tissue, a bottle, or whatever is needed and give it to the parent for the baby. School-aged children may be encouraged to read or sing to the new sibling, or to teach the child a new skill. Mullin and Johnson (1999) even advocated assigning a second social worker to the family to work solely with the children already there both before the new adoptee's arrival and postplacement, although that may be excessive if the parents have already reviewed the potential adoption effectively with the child(ren).

Typically, those who intend to adopt prefer to begin their parenting experience with an infant. Twenty years ago and more, being a single mother was seriously frowned upon by most of society, with the result that many unwed young women in that position gave their newborn child up for adoption. Although it may have been emotionally painful, they could, and often did, rationalize their action as providing the opportunity for a better life for the child than they could possibly provide. This meant that most of the children available for adoption *were* infants, and there were relatively few attempts to disrupt the adoption before it was finalized. Among pregnant white women, 19 percent gave up their babies at birth for adoption in 1965; by 1988, that percentage had dropped to 3 percent of the women (Evan B. Donaldson Adoption Institute, 2000). In a study of 177 pregnant or postpartum adolescents, all of them with unplanned pregnancies,

> the adolescent who is most likely to release for adoption perceives that she has a number of alternatives to early child rearing. She is likely to have thought a lot about what she will be doing in the future, plans to continue her schooling, and believes that ideally women should become mothers in their 20s. (Donnelly & Voydanoff, 1991, p. 408)

Of that sample, only twenty-four , or 13 percent, planned to release their babies, which supports the direction of the Donaldson Institute findings.

Child welfare agencies, in addition, operated on the principle that "efforts should be made to find a family similar to the child's racial, ethnic, cultural and religious background" (Barth & Berry, 1988, p. 7). This was reinforced by the 1972 policy adopted by the National Association of Black Social Workers (NABSW) in which they expressed vehement opposition to the placement of black children in white homes (Adoption, 1993). Although the NABSW recognized that many more black children were in need of a home than there were black families willing and able to take them in as foster or adoptive children, the organization's members were concerned that the children would lose their cultural ties and be unprepared to deal with the racism that existed then, and that continues in many venues today. It was thought that the Multiethnic Placement Act of 1994, amended two years later with the Interethnic Adoption Provisions, would reduce the problem of interracial placements, but the controversy continued even as such placements were made[3] (Adoption Controversies, 1999).

Changes in Practice

The traditional policies no longer dominate placement for a number of reasons. Today, relatively fewer infants are available and more disruptions, mostly in change of mind about finalizing the termination of parental rights (TPR) to facilitate the adoption by others. Similarity between the child's background and that of the prospective new family is less emphasized. Indeed, a series of statutes passed between 1974 (Child Abuse Prevention and Treatment Act, P.L. 93-247) and 2003 (Keeping Children and Families Safe Act, amended, P.L. 108-36) have made such "matching" illegal and ineligible for federal funds (NAIC, 2003b), although private agencies not receiving such funds may not be bound by this policy (see Figure 1.1). The Indian Child Welfare Act, enacted in 1978, is exempt from this policy, however. There are negative aspects to this exception though, if no one in the tribe is willing to adopt a child or if abused or neglected children are forced to remain in foster care, thus giving them lesser rights than other children (Dwyer, 2003).

Another changed factor has been the increase, sometimes at the behest (or demand) of the adoption placement agency, of some form of "open adoption." "Open adoption" permits ongoing contact between the biological parent(s), usually the mother, and the child who has been placed for adoption. The degree of contact may vary from the virtual minimum of the adoptive parents sending a photo of the child every year and the mother sending a birthday card to the child to the maximum frequent visits by the mother to the child combined with continuing interaction with the adoptive parents. "Open adoption" will be discussed in more detail in a later chapter.

In addition, there is increasing pressure to move children out of foster care into permanent homes and families. In some situations this has met with a concomitant increase in adoption disruptions. (It should be remembered, however, that even if the disruption rate is 15 or 20 percent, that means that 80 to 85 percent of the adoptions are not disrupted and are, presumably, at least, moderately successful.) By the time some of these children are eligible for adoption, they may have been in several foster homes or may be teenagers. In either case, they may well have potential problems in attaching themselves to the new adoptive family (Kirby & Hardesty, 1998). One study of postadoption experiences for the children and families created in this way found mixed results depending not only on the age and needs of the children, but access to support services and, interestingly, whether the family lived in a rural community or a more densely populated one (McDonald, Propp, & Murphy, 2001). The 159 children studied, many with special needs, were from a variety of racial/ethnic backgrounds, and had been placed for adoption at age 1.7 to 12.8 years (average 7.7 years), and 97 percent

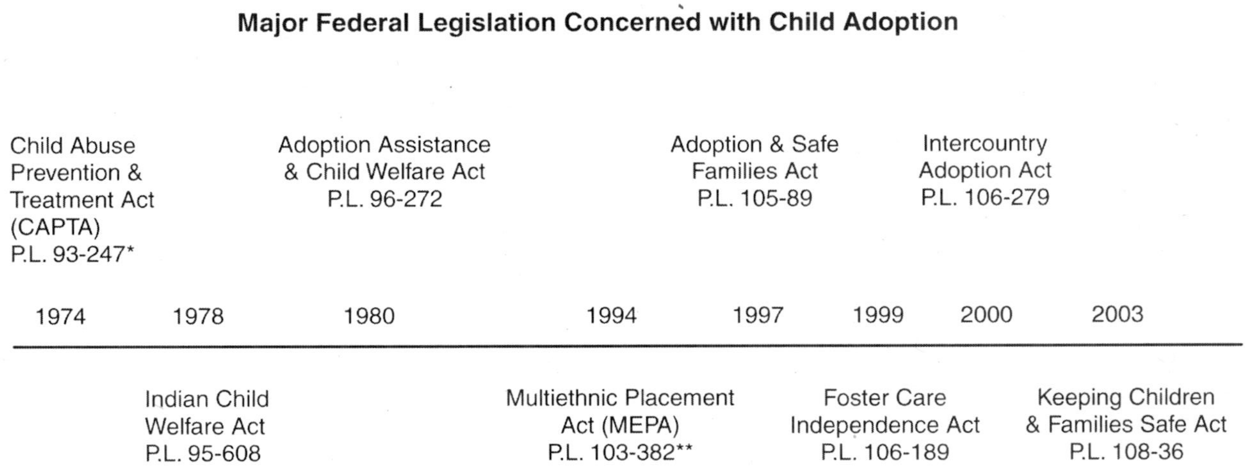

Major Federal Legislation Concerned with Child Adoption

	Adoption Assistance & Child Welfare Act P.L. 96-272	Adoption & Safe Families Act P.L. 105-89	Intercountry Adoption Act P.L. 106-279	Keeping Children & Families Safe Act P.L. 108-36
1974	1978	1980	1994	1997	1999	2000	2003

Child Abuse Prevention & Treatment Act (CAPTA) P.L. 93-247* — 1974

Indian Child Welfare Act P.L. 95-608 — 1978

Multiethnic Placement Act (MEPA) P.L. 103-382** — 1994

Foster Care Independence Act P.L. 106-189 — 1999

*CAPTA amended in 1978, 1984, 1988, 1992, 1996

**MEPA amended 1996

FIGURE 1.1. Federal adoption laws. *Source:* National Adoption Information Clearinghouse (2003b, October).

had been in their adoptive families for eighteen to twenty-four months. The majority of their responding parents tended to report that the caregiving experience had been relatively positive, that the children had contributed positively to the family, and that, for most of the respondents, support services had been available. The most negative factors were a child having multiple special needs, later age at placement, and living in a rural community. As will be discussed, should the prospective parents choose to adopt an older child, these possibilities need to be anticipated, recognized, and dealt with therapeutically (and promptly) to avert further damage to the children.

The Child's Past, Present, and Future

In any adoption, domestic or international, the prospective parents should have access to as much of the child's history as possible. What kind of pre- and postnatal care has the child had? Did the mother take drugs, overindulge in alcohol, or have HIV? Is there a known genetic disorder that has been biologically transmitted to the child? If the child is not an infant, has he or she been subjected to abuse? Has the child been moved from one foster home to another? Has the child been housed in an orphanage? For how long? It is critically important that adoption agencies provide this information in full and before the child is placed in the new home. (Instances of where this policy has not been followed are discussed under the heading of "Wrongful Adoption" in Chapter 3.) Not only will such information help the adoptive parents to anticipate or deal more effectively with problems the child may have, but it will also enable them to answer questions the child may ask about his or her biological parents—hopefully with tact, as the occasion or facts may demand.

Among the critical tasks that all children face are the development of a basic sense of trust (Erikson, 1950) and of a sense of homeostasis (Shapiro, Shapiro, & Paret, 2001b), especially for those who have been moved from one "home" to another; the development of an attachment relationship between the child and parent(s), which again may be more difficult if the child has been with more than one family; and the development of a sense of identity, which may vary with age when adopted (and later) and whether the child comes from a background similar to or different from the adoptive family in terms of race, ethnicity, or religion.

Certain children, most often following months or years of severe neglect and abuse as well as multiple placements and caregivers, develop gaps in their development that impede their readiness and ability to form attachments with their adoptive families, no matter how loving and committed those families are. (Hughes, 1999, p. 542)

Clearly, these children will need professional help, and the parents will also need professional support if the adoption is not to be disrupted.

If they have experienced environments that were risk laden for social, emotional, or cognitive development, they may have "deficits in their capacity for attachment relationships and possess a limited capacity for important explorations of relationships and the external world" (Shapiro, Shapiro, & Paret, 2001a). Brodzinsky, Smith, and Brodzinsky (1998) provide a thoughtful and thorough look at how children of varying backgrounds or in different stages of adoption adjust to adoption, and recognize the many factors that must be considered. Although some biological children may have difficulty mastering these developmental tasks, virtually all authors agree that the challenge may be increased for adopted children, especially if they are past early infancy at the time of placement. It becomes imperative then for parents to help their children to develop a resilient personality, a high level of personal discipline and sense of responsibility, a sense of focus, "a commitment to life, and a philosophical framework within which personal experiences can be interpreted with meaning and hope, even at life's seemingly most hopeless moments" (Schwartz, 1994, p. 205).

Domestic versus International Adoptions

In addition to the dwindling number of infants available for adoption in this country, and concerns about how truly permanent terminations of parental rights are, it may be that the adoptive couple does not meet the criteria of whatever domestic adoption agencies are available to them. In many cases, this is because the prospective parents are over or under a certain age, or are of different religious faiths. These factors do not appear to matter in most of the international adoption settings. It may also be that the only children the domestic agency can, or is willing to, place with them is a special needs child or an older one who may have been in and out of a few or several foster homes. These are all situations that may encourage the would-be parents to think of an international adoption.

Whether the prospective parents ultimately decide to adopt a child born in the United States or one born elsewhere, they also must decide whether to adopt through a private intermediary or through an adoption agency. Whichever they choose, they need to make every possible effort to ascertain the legitimacy and ethics of the intermediary or the agency, in order to reduce the risks of adoption disruption. Answering an advertisement placed by a pregnant woman in, e.g., *USA Today* or on the Internet, can lead to unanticipated grief, costs, and perhaps even legal liability. The case of the "Internet Twins," to be discussed, illustrates this type of problem.

The risks mentioned earlier have clearly contributed to the move of many prospective parents to consider international rather than domestic adoption. Although it is rare that a newborn can be adopted internationally, it is possible, depending on the country, to adopt an infant or a toddler. Many of the same questions about pre- and postnatal care, and other possible problems, can be raised with these children and older ones, as they are with domestic adoptions, but the optimism of most would-be adopters somehow creates the belief that such difficulties can be handled more effectively with children from overseas.

Perhaps the fact that the biological parents are unlikely to seek to reclaim the child, as they might in a domestic adoption, contributes to that more positive view. The greater certainty that the birth parents' rights are truly terminated in international adoptions eliminates what has become an increasing source of anxiety to some adoptive parents in the United States. In addition, the absence of a national putative father registry that would reduce belated contests over adoption and "the increasing acceptance and practice of open adoptions" are seen as factors that contribute to the increase in international adoptions (Fleisher, 2003, p. 172).

If the child is near preschool age or older, the prospective parents should be able to obtain a medical history and also possibly a videotape that can be shown to an American pediatrician for diagnosis of possible medical problems[4] (Nicholson, 2002). The preadoption videos are presently available from some sources in Russia and Eastern Europe, and their detection accuracy with respect to moderate or serious developmental delay is fair (Boone, Hostetter, & Weitzman,

2003). Although clearly not definitive as to problems, the videos might, at least, give the prospective parents and their doctors some idea of what kind of help may be needed most. As we know in domestic adoption as well as international, a child's difficulties vary with age as well as exposure to health problems and life experiences, however brief they may be.

Adoptive parents should be aware that the child will likely know no English, or a very few words at best, so that communication may be a problem for at least the early months of their new family. (It might help if the prospective parents learned a few useful phrases in the child's native language, of course.) Whether the child has experienced satisfactory care in an orphanage or has been kept in a crib although well past walking age, and whether he or she has bonded with anyone in the home country who will now be sorely missed, are also factors that will affect the child's adjustment to the new family (Groza, Ryan, & Cash, 2003; Judge, 2003).

Yet another issue that arises more frequently in international adoptions is ethnicity. Thousands of Asian children are being adopted in the United States annually, and usually by Caucasians, not Asians. Although this may not raise eyebrows in most of our larger cities and suburbs, the outcome may be somewhat different in some smaller communities and in those where the population tends to be rather homogeneous. Prospective parents need to be conscious of the kind of reception a child may get, not only from extended family, but also from schoolmates, in their community (Bergquist, Campbell, & Unrau, 2003; Rosettenstein, 1995; Shapiro, Shapiro, & Paret, 2001a; Vonk, 2001; Vonk, Simms, & Nackerud, 1999). As Vonk (2001) put it, transracial/cultural adoptive parents (TRA)

> who are sensitive to and aware of race, ethnicity, and culture are thought to be more able to help their children cope successfully with related issues. Racial awareness also may help parents understand the importance of recognizing their child's race and of fostering their child's identification with his or her race. Racial awareness is important in its own right, but also because without it, parents may not understand the value of multicultural planning and survival skills. (p. 250)

Support groups are available for such diverse families. Many of them hold a picnic or other social gatherings one or more times a year to celebrate, for example, the country of origin's national day, or some special rites. Indeed, where economically feasible, many of the parents plan to take their children to visit the native country when they are older adolescents, perhaps even to find the community or family from which they came originally (Schwartz & Kaslow, 2003).

TYING ADOPTION TO ADOPTION DISRUPTION

As should be apparent from the preceding pages, adoption can be a risky matter, whether domestic or international in origin. Having biological children can also be risky; genetic disorders may occur, or damage to the fetus can occur during pregnancy that is not apparent until after the child is born or even a few months old. As grief provoking as these occurrences may be, the child remains with the parents, and the parents usually do everything they can to cope with the problem. In the case of adopted children, some parents feel an omnipresent threat of disruption, or the possibility they have assumed a role they cannot fulfill. Sometimes these are the tragic instances when the adopted child and the adoptive parents part company by judicial ruling, before or after they have legally become a family. These events happen for many reasons, which are explored in some detail.

Chapter 2

Adoption Disruptions

Adoption *disruptions* are technically adoptions that are undone before they are finalized. This may occur for several reasons, including the changed views toward adoption and its alternatives over the past two centuries. Also, legislative and judicial factors are involved, particularly prejudices that are revealed in statutes and court rulings of which the petitioners and even judges may not even be aware.

TYPES AND CAUSES OF DISRUPTIONS

Adoptions disruptions occur for many reasons. Some are more pertinent to private or adoption agency placements, and some to the outcome of foster care placements. As will be seen, sometimes the interests and needs of the children may conflict with those of adults. Unfortunately, in too many cases the children's rights are not adequately represented, as not all jurisdictions mandate that the child be represented by a separate child advocate or guardian-ad-litem. It is the position here that children in the foster care or adoption system *should* have a voice in what happens to them, an informed voice that will be heard in the courtroom. "Informed" refers to the fact that the child's representative will have met the child, will have all the facts related to the child's background and caretaking, and will also have knowledge of the child's development. Children are people, not packages, and are entitled to be placed in accordance with what is truly in their "best interests," although preferably without violating anyone else's valid interests.

Unlike adoption, parenthood via sexual intercourse is not always intentional. It may be accidental, the product of rape, or, in some cases, purposeful. Even if the parties *do* intend to conceive initially,

When Adoptions Go Wrong
© 2006 by The Haworth Press, Inc. All rights reserved.
doi:10.1300/5780_02

however, their circumstances may change so that the baby's arrival is no longer the source of delight that had been anticipated. This can lead to placing the child for adoption. If the adults' circumstances change again, there may be adoption disruption.

Disruption may occur before final adoption papers are signed due to:

- revocation of maternal consent;
- unmarried father's intervention;
- differences in time period to final adoption; and
- greed.

Additional problems, which may arise from inadequate social services, foster care, and incompatibility of child and adoptive parents, are discussed in the next chapter.

Revocation of Maternal Consent

As already mentioned, a few decades ago, when single and/or unwed motherhood were definitely frowned upon, young women more often placed their children for adoption and rarely withdrew their consent. Indeed, many of these young women spent their pregnancies in Salvation Army care or similar shelters, receiving appropriate prenatal care, but usually with the understanding that their babies were to be placed for adoption. They may or may not have received balanced counseling to help them think through the situation, but at least gave one another some support during their months together.

Other cases, however, have had less constructive outcomes. Too often, if a teenage girl gets pregnant, she may keep that news to herself or even deny it to herself, and ultimately in her panic—or at the behest of her parents—give the baby up for adoption. A couple waiting to adopt a baby happily welcomes the child. Then, for whatever reason, the girl changes her mind and wants the baby back.

In 1980-1981, when Pennsylvania law, for example, allowed the mother six months to withdraw her consent to adopt, a notorious case involved Rachael Marie Yack, who the courts ordered returned to her biological parents when the child was more than a year old (Schwartz, 1983). The mother was a high school senior when she gave birth in March 1980. Toward the end of the year-long legal battle that followed, first the adoption (contested by the unmarried father on the day the child went home with the Yacks), and then the withdrawal of consent by the mother (two weeks after placement), the courts even placed the child in foster homes until appeals could be decided. As one columnist put it at the time, "The baby is shifted back and forth like a tired toy. This is done in the name of justice and human concern" (Storck, 1981, p. B1). This was yet another example of a child being viewed as property rather than as a person, and of her best interests not being considered. Matters were not helped by delays and conflicts in judicial rulings.

Pertman (2000) offers the story of a young woman who was strongly pressured by her case worker in a residential "shelter" to give up her baby for adoption, did so under the pressure, and immediately after tried to revoke her consent. It apparently took her eighteen months to recover her son, the result of a legal "fluke." She indicated that she regretted the pain she caused his adoptive parents, but, of course, was greatly gratified to have her son back. She went on to become a mental health counselor, and apparently the adoptive parents had enough resilience after this legal battle to adopt again. That case occurred more than twenty years ago, but Pertman also presented more current stories of how unmarried pregnant women are handled, pressured, and sometimes stigmatized.[1]

Today, being an unwed mother is not held in as much disdain and giving the baby up for adoption is not pressed as much. However, the female's rights to make that decision if she is a minor are the same as if she was an adult, even though, in most states, she would not be allowed as a minor to consent to having sex, to make a decision to have an abortion, or to select which medical treatment she will have during pregnancy, if any at all (Durcan & Appell, 2001). The question about keeping the child or not varies to some degree with the circumstances of impregnation. If the girl was raped, then more than likely she will give the baby up for adoption (if she doesn't have an abortion first or commit neonaticide). She would see the baby as a constant reminder of that horrendous experience, and that would undoubtedly affect her caretaking of and attachment to the child.

In other cases, the girl/young woman became pregnant as a result of consensual sexual activity, deliberately unprotected or not. If the mother is still in her mid-teens, family pressures or the young woman's own thinking about her situation may lead her to place her child for adoption. If she does not have professional guidance, however, she may decide at the last minute—*after* the child has been placed, that she simply cannot go through with it and she revokes her consent. Whether or not her state's laws mention minor-age birth mothers, "the general rule is that the minority of a birth parent will not free her from the consequences of her relinquishment, although had the same young woman entered into a commercial contract, she could void it at any time" (Durcan & Appell, 2001, p. 74).

Perhaps, as in the Baby Jessica case to be discussed, the mother has been belatedly exposed to an antiadoption group and changes her mind. Or perhaps she has belatedly determined that she wants access to the child *after* adoption, i.e., have an "open" adoption, or else she will withdraw her consent. By this time, the baby may well have been with the adoptive parents for a few to several months. The decision to place the child may have been gut-wrenching for her; the revocation is equally gut-wrenching to the would-be parents and, to varying extents, the baby.

Unmarried Father's Intervention

In some cases of rape, or if the young woman had been involved with a male who is no longer part of her life, she decides to place the child for adoption. She does not tell the alleged father, for any of a number of reasons. Perhaps he finds out, decides he wants custody for whatever reason he may assert, and she threatens to revoke her consent to thwart him. What rights does he have, if any?

Delay or disruption of an adoption caused by actions of the birth mother in misidentifying the father, deliberately or otherwise, or simply in not notifying him of the child's birth, often set the stage for the unmarried father's intervention. Thus when he finally becomes aware of his child's existence and tries to intervene in the adoption, before or after the child's legal adoption, a protracted legal battle may occur. Questions may be raised as to his emotional and/or financial support of the mother during her pregnancy and after, as well as whether he has made any attempt to take care of the baby. The outcome of the conflict may rest on whether or not the final court decision considers what is in the child's "best interests." The Baby Jessica case of the early 1990s, in particular, illustrates the effects of the belated intervention of the biological father in an adoption case as well as the complications in statutes that may affect the ultimate outcome of this type of case.

The "Baby Jessica" Case

Baby Jessica was born in Iowa on February 8, 1991, and her prospective adoptive parents (the DeBoers) were granted custody pending her adoption about two weeks later (February 25). In this case, the mother, Cara Clausen, signed away her rights to the baby about forty hours after delivery, and the man she *identified* as father signed off on his rights four days later. She had received no counseling about her rights, including her right to revoke the consent up to seventy-two hours after delivery, and neither she nor the alleged father was present in court, although they had been notified of the hearing at which their rights were to be terminated[2] (Resnik, 1996).

Glazer (1993), writing while this case was in progress, but before the passage of the Uniform Adoption Act, apparently interviewed Cara Clausen Schmidt, eliciting information that may or may not ever have reached a judge's desk in all the appeals that ultimately occurred. She wrote:

> To avoid the kind of intense pressure Cara Schmidt says she experienced when the DeBoers' lawyer had her sign the consent papers from her hospital bed, a neutral party—such as a judge, court referee or the birth parent's own lawyer—would preside over consents. (p. 1052)

The then-proposed code would have had her consent negated because it was granted in the presence of an interested party before the allowable seventy-two-hour "change of mind period" would have elapsed.

The DeBoers promptly moved, with Baby Jessica, back to their home in Michigan. At about the same time, the biological mother attended a meeting of an antiadoption group and changed her mind. Two days later, she informed a former boyfriend, Daniel Schmidt, that she thought *he* was Jessica's father and he filed a request (on March 27, 1991) that the (false) paternal termination of rights be vacated, followed by his filing an affidavit of paternity. Jessica was then forty-eight days old. When Jessica was about eight months old (September 1991), Schmidt filed proof of his paternity (99.9 percent certainty) and the adoptive parents filed a petition to terminate his rights because he was an unfit parent. That was based on his alleged record with other children he had fathered. (Question: Why did it take Schmidt so many months to file the proof of his paternity?)

In December 1991, the Iowa District Court denied the DeBoers' adoption petition, acknowledging their exemplary parenting but finding that they had not presented clear and convincing evidence of Schmidt's unfitness. The court ordered them to return the child to Iowa, and to her biological parents (Resnik, 1996). The DeBoers refused.

Hollinger (1995) raised the question of why the court delayed an immediate hearing, and why the guardian-ad-litem ultimately appointed for the baby did not press for a prompter determination. Both would have been in the child's best interests, since any move from the DeBoers to the Schmidts would have occurred when she was younger and somewhat less attached to the DeBoers. In addition, Hollinger raised the question of which couple really offered a better model as parents: Cara Clausen (Schmidt) who lied about her pregnancy and the identity of the child's father, and Daniel Schmidt, who allegedly had failed to support any of his prior children or their mothers (DuRocher, 1994), or the DeBoers who had a stable relationship and comfortable home to which to welcome a child. The differences between the two possible homes was not the key issue here; however, Hollinger correctly raised the question of time delays, which played a far more critical role.

Almost a year later, after their appeal to the Iowa Supreme Court was remanded to the district court, they were again ordered to return Jessica to her mother in Iowa. They again refused and, in January 1993, a bench warrant was issued by the Iowa court for their arrest. The DeBoers persisted, taking their case through the Michigan courts unsuccessfully (State Bar of Michigan, 2001). By now, Jessica was more than two years old. The Michigan circuit court sought to have jurisdiction under provisions of the Uniform Child Custody Jurisdiction Act or UCCJA (Resnik, 1996, p. 370), but was overruled by both the court of appeals and the Michigan Supreme Court (*DeBoer v. Schmidt,* 1993a). The UCCJA, incidentally, required state courts to enforce custody orders of other states, so that this interstate conflict should not have happened (Hollinger, 1995, n. 3). An appeal to the U.S. Supreme Court was denied (*DeBoer v. Schmidt,* 114 S. Ct. 11

[1993b]), and the DeBoers were thereby forced to surrender Jessica to Daniel Schmidt, a complete stranger to the child.

The Iowa court held, and the appellate courts agreed, that considering Jessica's best interests was irrelevant and a legal error (Scarnecchia, 1994). Her best interests were apparently not represented by any legal counsel solely on her behalf at any judicial level, except at one early point when the guardian-ad-litem had apparently not pressed for the transfer issue to be settled promptly. There was also apparently no effort to have a transition period so that Jessica could at least meet her father and become somewhat acquainted with him before being moved to his home. Her biological parents had married during this time, but clearly Jessica had also bonded with her adoptive parents in this period (Weaver-Catalana, 1995). Her removal from the latter, sobbing at the separation from the only parents she knew, was shown on prime-time television. From a psychological point of view, given the number of appeals, understandable to a degree from the DeBoers' perspective, and their slow resolution, the least that could have been done for the child was to order a supervised transition program. She was, after all, almost three years old by then, and would have had little understanding of why she was being separated from them. Unfortunately for the child, it seems that no provision was made for any continuing contact between the DeBoers and the Schmidts.

The Schmidts were divorced in 2000 and share custody of Jessica, known as Anna after her return to the Schmidts (Associated Press Online, 2003). Daniel Schmidt was apparently injured in 1998 and has not worked since, although Anna and her younger sister live with him. Ten years after her return, in August 2003, Anna was reported to be doing well, and claimed not to recall the DeBoers, nor to want contact with them. Her father was quoted as saying, "No, we don't communicate with them. That's how we all prefer it" (Associated Press Online, 2003). Presumably the "we" refers to himself and his ex-wife, Cara, as well as Anna.

As an incidental note, the DeBoers were seen on the NBC *Today Show* on June 3, 2004 (NBC News Transcripts, 2004a) in connection with the removal of identical twin girls from their mother.[3] Apparently in conjunction with the Associated Press "update" on Jessica/Anna in 2003, the DeBoers had seen video footage of the girl the year before. The DeBoers understandably had a strong emotional response to this, but were pleased to see how well she seemed to be.

They expressed their continuing love for the child they called Jessica and wished her and her family well.

The Evan Scott Case

On the last day of 2004 yet another case came to public attention, this time on the *Today Show* (Associated Press, December 31, 2004; NBC News transcript, December 31, 2004b). Evan Scott, age three and a half, was being transferred from his would-be adoptive parents in Florida to his biological mother for a "transitional visit" before being placed in her custody permanently (unless further court rulings occur). (Following this visit, Evan was to return to the Scotts for a week prior to returning permanently to his biological mother and her husband in Illinois.) His biological mother, Amanda Hopkins, had decided to place Evan with Dawn and Gene Scott upon his birth as the child's father, to whom she was not married, was supposedly going to prison for twenty years for attempted murder (NBC News Transcripts, 2004b). There was no mention in either the AP story or the *Today* interview of the father having given her emotional or financial support during her pregnancy. (There are some similarities here to the Baby Emily case, also in Florida, which is presented in the next chapter.)

The Scotts brought Evan home shortly after his birth in May 2001. They anticipated acquiring legal custody of him in August that year. Initial attempts to secure the father's consent as well were unanswered, but in July, the father, Steven A. White Jr., filed for immediate custody of his son, a motion opposed by the Scotts unsuccessfully. The Scotts' attorney at that time had apparently voiced the opinion that White's consent would not be necessary as he had not met Florida's requirements for filing for paternity (NBC News Transcripts, 2004b). That was overruled in September 2002, and White began to have supervised visits with Evan that November, as well as taking the child on visits to his parents' home in New Hampshire later on (Brice, 2005). Evan called him "Daddy Steve." Hopkins, who had supported the Scotts' adoption of the boy until White's intervention, withdrew her consent in September 2004 for fear that a judge *would* grant White custody. In late December 2004, a judge awarded custody to Hopkins (now Hopkins Johnson), and also ordered that White be given liberal visitation rights, although apparently no mention was made of giving the same rights to the Scotts, the only full-time parents Evan has ever known. Not only that, but the Scotts were not even given standing to appeal for his custody. They appealed to both the appellate court and the governor of Florida. On January 6, 2005, the judge ruled again that the change of custody process must continue and, further, that Evan's name be changed to Evan Johnson (Brice, 2005). The U. S. Supreme Court declined to hear the appeal on January 10. The exchange took place on January 15 in Jacksonville, Florida (Word, 2005). The history of the case, including allegations by the four parental figures about one another's intents and actions, was the subject of a one-hour *Larry King Live* telecast on January 27, 2005, and of a half-hour telecast on *Dateline NBC* on January 30, 2005.

Several questions arise in this case, most of them concerned with the basis for the ruling giving White partial custody in September 2002, when the Scotts' original attorney believed that he had no standing to file a paternity claim. Furthermore, there is certainly a question about the prison term he was supposed to serve, but apparently is not doing so. Although the judge who ordered the "transitional visit" prior to permanent transfer is to be commended for doing so, a question certainly arises as to why the Scotts were then excluded from filing for custody, or from having visitation rights.

Differences in Time Period to Final Adoption

In dealing with the biological mother alone, differences occur from state to state, and even county to county within a state, in the number of days or months she has to sign an agreement to or withdraw her consent from the adoption. If the period is as long as a year, or even six months, and she withdraws consent in the latter part of that period, the child is old enough to have become emotionally attached to the caretaking parents and to become distressed if removed from them. In the past decade, several states have shortened the time period, with New Jersey, for example, terminating parental rights three days after a consent form has been signed, and Pennsylvania now limiting a change of mind to thirty days (Worden, 2004). The time limits for alleged fathers to enter their claims are obviously in a state of flux at this time as the various states work out putative father registries and time limits for asserting parental rights for unmarried fathers.

Greed

Money may or may not be "the root of all evil," but it can certainly contribute to adoption disruption. The biological mother may choose her child's adoptive parents primarily on the basis of what they will pay her to surrender the child (more likely to occur in cases of private placement). (This is one kind of greed that is exemplified by the case of the "Internet Twins.") However, she may also make her decision based on what benefits may accrue to her (more likely in agency placement). Such a case was seen on national television in late April 2004 (Barbara Walters, *20/20*) when a sixteen-year-old girl, apparently with the approval of the agency with which she was involved, interviewed five sets of prospective parents and made her choice on the basis of which one would give her *and* her extended family the most access to the child after adoption (Carter, 2004; Lubrano, 2004). Although this case did not appear to be based on financial greed, it certainly seemed to represent a kind of emotional greed, a desire to "eat one's cake and have it, too."

The "Internet Twins"

Blatant greed was a key factor in upsetting the adoption by the Allens in California of twin girls born in June 2000. They had responded to the availability of the children for adoption, for a fee, which had been advertised on the Internet. About two months after the girls went to the Allens, the mother appeared and asked to have a visit with the children. She removed them, ostensibly for a private but brief local visit, and did not bring them home again. Prior to the "visit," she had agreed to their adoption by a British couple, the Kilshaws, for a fee double that paid by the Allens. She and the Kilshaws went to Arkansas, claiming to be residents there, and the Kilshaws were declared the adoptive parents. They immediately flew home to Wales with the twins. The Allens, meanwhile, were attempting to get the children back. This came to the attention of British authorities, who removed the twins from the Kilshaws and placed them in a foster home. They were subsequently returned to the United

States so that the adoption by the Kilshaws could be overturned, and then faced yet another family placement (Hoge, 2001). They were in their fourth home before the age of eight months, were subsequently adopted by foster parents in Missouri, and in December 2004 were in danger of being moved again depending on the outcome of a then-pending court action involving their biological mother.

Tranda Wecker (the twins' biological mother), now remarried, has somewhat belatedly sought to reclaim the children (Anonymous, 2004a). As has been mentioned in a number of court hearings, the twins have actually spent only fifty-two days of their almost four years of life in her care (Bryant, 2004). The courts have already terminated the biological father's rights, with his agreement (Bryant, 2004) and the first of a series of nonpublic hearings regarding Tranda Wecker Conley's rights was to occur on July 8, 2004[4] (Salter, 2004). However, on that date, the judge who had originally terminated the mother's rights removed himself from the case (KSDK, July 9, 2004).

This case threatens to be in the courts for at least another year or two, with apparently little thought being given to the effects on the little girls of all the moves they have experienced, or the bonds they have presumably developed with the family that has cared for them for most of the past three years. Even as young as the girls are, they may have unconsciously decided to bond with each other as the only consistent figures in their environment.

Incidentally, similar cases of greed and the misuse of the Internet to "promote" adoption can be found (Pertman, 2000). In one horrific case, a birth mother had placed her baby up for auction to the highest bidder on eBay. This seems incredible. Fortunately, the auction house removed the offer before a sale could be concluded (Pertman, 2000, p. 187).

SUMMARY

The focus of attention in this chapter is on the ways in which the choices and decisions of the biological parents can enhance or disrupt adoption. The interdependence of the first three factors presented, pertaining to disrupted adoptions, should be self-evident. Although the biological parents should clearly have time to consider their options with respect to their child, it is also realistic to place a limit on that time so that there is less harm done to the child in terms of relationships. The fourth factor, greed, is also related to biological parental consent to adoption, although for most people the idea of "virtually" offering one's child to the highest "bidder" is incredible.

Chapter 3

Other Causes Contributing to Adoption Disruptions

Festinger found three reasons most cited for disruptions: (1) expectations of the families and fear that they could not cope with the child's behaviors; (2) the children's expectations which *they* felt were not being met; and (3) the nature of the family's motivation to adopt (1986, p. 39). She concluded that not only was more agency service needed to prevent disruptions, but also a better quality of service. However, some of the factors contributing to problems in adoption stem from ineffectual social welfare services because of overloaded staff or wrongful practices, and misuse or abuse of the foster care system. Our interdisciplinary examination now shifts to these and other related problems.

INADEQUATE SOCIAL SERVICES

Welfare agency services are inadequate when they fail to meet the real needs of the children they place, the biological parents who may have lost custody of their children only temporarily, and the foster/adoptive parents with whom children may be placed. All of these people need agency support in some form. Certainly the foster and/or adoptive parents need full information about the children's background and experiences and any special health or other problems. Thought needs to be given to the effects on the children of the decisions made by caseworkers and other agency personnel. Too often, not all perspectives are considered in decision making, as in the "Gregory K" case.

When Adoptions Go Wrong
© 2006 by The Haworth Press, Inc. All rights reserved.
doi:10.1300/5780_03

The Case of "Gregory K"

A quite unusual outcome of a foster care placement should be noted for a number of reasons. Gregory Kingsley had been in foster care for more than two years when, at age eleven, he filed a petition to terminate his biological parents' rights in the parent-child relationship. He had his own privately retained legal counsel. As one author put it, "If children are citizens, not chattel . . ." they should have the right to sue in their own best interests (Day, 2000, p. 652). Almost six months later, his petition was granted and his adoption by his foster parents was permitted (Russ, 1993). This was subsequently upset by Florida's appellate court on the grounds that, as an unemancipated minor, Gregory did not have the standing to bring a suit in his own name (Dolgin, 1997). However, the appellate court also found the error to be harmless and permitted him to terminate his parents' rights so that he could be adopted by the Russ couple who had been his foster parents (Harding, 2001).

This case developed from the following events: Gregory was born in 1980. His parents had separated when he was four years old. He spent the next few years with his father, who had a substance-abuse problem and who was both abusive to and neglectful of the boy. When Gregory was nine, Florida's welfare services removed him from his father's custody and placed him and a brother with his mother. That arrangement lasted for five months, at which time she voluntarily placed the boys in foster care for almost a year. Gregory's next reunion with his mother lasted only a couple of months, at which time he was involuntarily placed in foster care as a dependent child. His mother was found to have substance-abuse problems, paid little attention to her children, and neglected them, among other problems (Russ, 1993). Gregory was placed for a time in a group setting, during which time his mother neither visited nor communicated with him.

In October 1991, he was placed with the Russ family, and a few months later the Department of Health and Rehabilitative Services (DHRS) decided to seek termination of his parents' rights, to the delight of the boy. Six weeks later, the agency reversed its position and sought to reunite the boy with his biological parents. A guardian-ad-litem had been appointed, but apparently never communicated with Gregory (yet another weakness in the system). Ultimately, the boy obtained an attorney and filed for termination of his parents' rights so that he could be adopted by his foster parents. His attorney, Jerri Blair, asserted, "It is HRS's [Health and Rehabilitative Services] position that children should never develop close emotional bonds with their foster parents" (Blair, 1993, p. 23). This seems a strange position for the agency to hold when a child needs to feel a bond and an attachment. His father voluntarily gave up his rights, but the mother did not. Gregory's right to sue then became the issue. Finally, he prevailed and was adopted, even changing his name to Shawn Russ to reflect his new life and new family.

Caseworker Problems

The services will also be inadequate when the caseworker has a case overload that makes it impossible for her (or him) to make each visit to the child's placement location both thorough and helpful. In Milwaukee, Wisconsin, for example, a suit was filed on behalf of more than a dozen plaintiffs (children) in the foster-care system because of abuse and neglect they suffered in out-of-home placements, infrequent caseworker contact with the children, lack of provision of background information on the child at placement, too frequent moves of children from one placement to another, and delays in placing the children in permanent homes *(Jeanine B. v. McCallum)*. The caseworkers at that time were each responsible for more than 100 children! Jeanine B., whose name is on the case, was a twelve-year-old who was moved among six different homes in a six-year period. In one of those homes, there were eleven other children, as well as a foster father who physically abused her. A settlement agreement between the plaintiffs and the agency was finally reached in 2002 after supplemental complaints had been filed. By the following year, the caseworkers' loads averaged 19.5 children per worker instead of more than 100, more placement information was available to foster parents at the time of placement (91 percent of data against 7 percent only a few years earlier), and the number of adoptions finalized in 2003 was more than double the number in 2001.

The services will be even more inadequate if the caseworker is not appropriately trained to do his or her job, or if the worker assigned to a particular case is frequently replaced. In Massachusetts, for example, the Department of Social Services has had too few professionally trained social workers, regarding its uncertified caseworkers as "social workers" simply because they work for the department (Kay, 2002). Even their time available for continuing education is limited due to the number of families and children each worker supervises. When these inadequacies of time and/or training occur, as will be seen in the Jackson boys' case to be discussed in the next chapter, tragedy can result.

Wrongful Adoption

Related to inadequate agency services are those cases termed "wrongful adoptions," the result of fraud or deliberate deceit by adoption agencies or some of their personnel. In the case of wrongful adoptions, substantial portions of relevant information are deliberately withheld. In the 1920s, when many modern adoption statutes were enacted, confidentiality and anonymity were key elements of the codes, with no information about the birth parents' health, or that of the child, to be released (Morgan, 1998). More than half a century later, this pattern was changed so that adopting parents *would* know the medical background of the children. Courts have recognized a duty to disclose known material information about a child's health and social background to prospective adoptive families. In the face of a breach of this duty, courts have held agencies liable and awarded adoptive families monetary damages (Freundlich & Peterson, 1998; also see Freundlich & Peterson, 1999).

These cases do not always result in disrupted adoptions, however, because by the time the parents have discovered the child's severe problems (e.g., mental retardation, ADHD, even psychosis) they have bonded with the child. The monetary damages awarded in tort actions not only "punish" the agency, but fund the extraordinary medical expenses and lifelong support that the parents will have to supply.

Kopels (1995) described a number of wrongful adoption cases, including one in which a seventeen-month-old boy, allegedly a healthy baby born to an eighteen-year-old unwed mother at a city hospital, had in fact been born to a thirty-one-year-old institutionalized mental patient with low intellectual functioning. The little boy functioned at a retarded level, suffered hallucinations, and was ultimately found to have Huntington's disease, which is genetically transmitted. The adoptive parents sued, and were the first to be awarded damages for the failure of the adoption agency to provide available health information[1] (*Burr v. Board of County Commissioners,* 1986).

Another boy, also allegedly healthy, suffered an epileptic seizure at age eleven and was found to be suffering from a congenitally transmitted degenerative nerve disorder. The condition was present at birth, and the county apparently had a notification, which it did not share with the adoptive parents, from a physician who said he could not make a prognosis of the boy's health. In a third case, a social worker did tell the prospective parents that there was a "possibility" of incest in the child's background that might produce some abnormalities. When a psychologist working with the child requested more information, the agency delivered a document which stated clearly that the child's parents were a seventeen-year-old boy and his thirteen-year-old sister. The agency finally admitted that it knew of the incestuous relationship when it first considered placing the child, but chose not to inform prospective adoptive parents.[2]

Morgan (1998) presents additional cases of tort actions with respect to wrongful adoption. These include intentional withholding of medical and psychological information, negligent misrepresentation, negligent nondisclosure and failure to investigate, and intentional infliction of emotional distress. A case in Pennsylvania, *Gibbs v. Ernst* (1994), was decided in favor of the plaintiffs regarding the last two of these offenses. The court held, in this case, "that an adoption agency has a duty to disclose fully and accurately to adoptive parents all relative nonidentifying information in its possession regarding the adoptee" (Morgan, 1998, p. 15), and also that the plaintiffs were entitled to be awarded damages for the "intentional infliction of emotional distress" (Morgan, 1998, p. 16).

In addition, there are also cases of deliberate fraud or withholding of information in international adoptions. Although the child is reported to be healthy, and looks that way in photos and videos, there may, in fact, be medical conditions that are known in the native country and of which the adopting parents are made aware, sometimes in the language of the country of origin, only *after* they have brought the child into their home and hearts (Schwartz & Kaslow, 2003).

Although these cases may not result in legally disrupted adoptions, they certainly cause disruption and distress within the family. In some cases, the child may have to be hospitalized because of violent or even psychotic behavior, effectively disrupting family life. The situation is not quite the same as in cases of parent-child incompatibility, in which the parents may know of the child's physical or intellectual needs at the time of adoption and then find themselves simply overwhelmed by these needs.

FOCUS ON FOSTER CARE

Large numbers of children are cared for by welfare agencies, and their adoption, in the absence of return to their biological families, is the focus of much recent legislation. When the potential adoptions fail, there are attempts to find out why this happens. In most cases, the research has involved agency placement and possibly foster care, and less frequently includes independent adoptions.

Researchers have found a consistent pattern over the years relevant to adoption disruptions and age at placement. Many of the studies have found that disruptions for children placed before school age were about 1.5 percent, while the percentage for children over age six when they were placed varied from 7 to 12 percent, and even higher in some studies (Barth & Berry, 1988; Festinger, 1986). A number of factors contribute to this situation. Multiple prior foster homes is one source of problems for the older children. It is more difficult for them to adjust to the new setting and become attached to the prospective adoptive parents. Many youngsters caught in this pattern had difficulty in dealing with separation and loss (Barth & Berry, 1988). Festinger reports

> when compared to children who were adopted, those whose placement [was] disrupted were more likely to have had a previous placement, had more placements of all sorts, and been placed in more families. . . . Their more checkered placement history suggests that these children exhibited more problems early on or developed them during their stay in care. (1986, p. 23)

Discontinuity of social service workers preparing the child and the family for placement, and lack of, postadoption support, were also found more frequently in adoption disruption (1986, pp. 36-37). Others in higher-rate disruption groups included groups of siblings, which would include at least one older child, and special needs children, who were and are also placed when they are older.

OTHER ISSUES AND IMPEDIMENTS

Children who have been removed from their biological parents and placed in foster care may languish there for years, despite recurring efforts to correct this situation. In most efforts to alter the long-term placement, social service systems and the courts attempt to return the children to the biological parents, ignoring the fact that crucial bonds have usually formed between the children and the ongoing caretakers "that cannot be disturbed without the same harm that comes from taking children from loving biological families" (Russ, 1993, p. 387). It is as if the children are property and have no rights of their own, a situation that was prevalent in the United States for several generations (Mason, 1994). Too often, there is no evidence of awareness that each case is different, whether by age of child at the time of placement, the reasons for placement, or whether the child has had any ongoing contact with the biological parents.[3]

Application of the Adoption and Safe Families Act

The Adoption and Safe Families Act of 1997 was one effort to correct the situation of children languishing in prolonged foster care, i.e., remove children from excessively long foster-care placements and either reunite them with their parents or make them available for adoption (when this would be in their "best interests"). Social service agencies would be required to "move to terminate parental rights when children had been in foster care for 15 out of the previous 22 months" (Kenyon et al., 2003, p. 572). In practice, however, not only is this rule not always followed as a matter of policy, but it may actually work at cross-purposes with other efforts, such as rehabilitation of an alcoholic mother (which can take longer than fifteen months) or release from prison of an incarcerated yet caring caretaking parent (Ross, 2004).

Some are concerned that this rule may be particularly difficult to implement in cases involving African-American children. They are disproportionately represented among those in foster care (Curtis & Denby, 2004). Caseworkers who participated in the Curtis and Denby study (2004) had a number of concerns: the speedy time frame, considering the nature of parental problems in the non-white population; placement of children with relatives who needed financial assistance to adopt them rather than continue as foster parents; overplacement of older children in group care or shelter settings; and poorly handled adoptions with inadequate postadoption support services. Curtis and Denby concluded that:

> The permanency focus of ASFA, including fiscal incentives to states for removing children from foster care and placing them in permanent settings and the provisions that may prompt swifter action by jurists to terminate parental rights, creates an environment in which the well-being of children vulnerable to family disruption is questionable. (2004, p. 78)

Another critic of AFSA, Ross (2004), points out that regardless of parental fitness or unfitness, statutory deadlines may interfere with a child's ultimate placement and best interests, as well as being exceeded in time for a variety of reasons.

However, there is another side to this debate. Heldman (2003) writes,

> For infants, the standard of terminating parental rights after fifteen months in foster care is far too long. Aside from the psychological damage that occurs from this lapse of time, the practical fact is that a child's chances for adoption decrease with age. Under current time frames, infants entering foster care will often be toddlers by the time they are freed for adoption, and thus will have missed out on their prime opportunity for successful adoptions. (p. 1020)

This Act (AFSA) clearly does not provide all the answers. Nor is it likely, given the atmosphere in the period when it was conceived and written, that there is much "wiggle room" for a judge to apply to an individual case. Even if there were, would every judge take advantage of such a clause?

Adoption by Homosexuals

A great deal of controversy surrounds adoption of children by gays and lesbians, although they may be accepted with slightly less "to-do" as foster parents. A national survey conducted by the Evan B. Donaldson Adoption Institute in 1999-2000 found that 60 percent of adoption agencies accepted applications from homosexuals, and about 40 percent of the agencies had placed children with gay or lesbian parents (Pertman, 2003). In most jurisdictions, sexual orientation is only one of several factors that the court might consider in deciding the eligibility of prospective adoptive parents (Greiner, 2004). After an extensive review of cases, however, Gesing (2004) concluded that, "The fact is, despite the victories of homosexual rights' activists throughout the United States, stereotypes against homosexuals and their ability to function as supportive, loving, and fit parents remain" (p. 896).

Although technically not an adoption disruption, in Florida, homosexuals are allowed to serve as foster parents, but are not allowed to adopt them, with removal from their care after a protracted period. This constitutes a wrench in the bonds of attachment similar to those developed with heterosexual foster parents, as explained. In the view of Reding (2003), this is a violation of the equal protection clause of the Fourteenth Amendment. Reding wrote that Florida's law denying homosexuals the right to adopt fails all three equal-protection tests (Reding, 2003). In sum, the Florida court ignored ongoing discrimination against gays and lesbians that is based on prejudice and ignored their ability to contribute to society, both in general and as parents. This prejudice was perhaps voiced most loudly in a child custody case, not an adoption, in which the couple was divorced. The mother was a homosexual and custodian of an eleven-year-old daughter, and the father had been convicted of the murder (second degree) of his first wife and served more than eight years in prison for his crime. In this case, *Ward v. Ward* (1996), the Florida court reversed the girl's custody apparently primarily, if not only, because of the mother's sexual orientation, and made the father her legal custodian despite his documented violent history. Unfortunately, the emphasis in the law and the courts that have reviewed the matter all focus on the homosexuality of the would-be parent and only rarely on the effects of a forced separation from that parent on the child.

A number of legal impediments exist involving adoption by homosexuals in several states. Florida, Utah, and Mississippi all have laws that make it difficult, if not impossible, for homosexuals to adopt. Other states permit adoption by a single homosexual individual, but not unmarried couples. In practice, this eliminates homosexual couples from adopting since they are not permitted to marry in most states. Utah's law, enacted in 2000, permits placement for adoption only with two heterosexual married adults. No such placement is permitted by same-sex couples, unmarried heterosexual couples, or single parents living with a significant other or a partner (Hong, 2003, p. 2). Hong views this as an impermissible state control on a person's ability to form a family, on a par with state limitations on private sexual activity that were declared unlawful by the U. S. Supreme Court in *Lawrence v. Texas* (2003, p. 11).

Gomes asserted that "What is truly harmful for children of gay parents is the lack of legal protection arising out of a failure to recognize same-sex marriage or to allow adoption by non-biological life partners" (2003, p. 15). Furthermore, the nonbiological parent usually cannot, under these laws, consent to emergency medical treatment or attend parent-teacher conferences, among other "privileges" usually accorded parents (p. 16). This issue gained visibility in 2003-2004 when homosexual marriages were legalized in Massachusetts and elsewhere. In that state, New York, Vermont, and the District of Columbia, on the other hand, the state's high courts have permitted adoption by lesbian and gay individuals or same-sex couples (Greiner, 2004).

If homosexuals are seen as fit to serve as foster parents for extended periods—in *Lofton v. Kearney* for more than ten years for some of their children—why are they not considered fit to adopt these children? By contrast, in a study of neonaticide, infanticide, and filicide (Schwartz & Isser, 2000), more than 150 cases were logged in the past decade in which *heterosexual* parents killed their children, and we are all too familiar with frequent cases of severe child abuse by *heterosexual* parents. Is it the type of sexual person one is that determines parenting quality?

Several studies have found that children adopted by homosexual parents are not adversely affected by the parents' orientation. In fact, the adults appear to divide parenting responsibilities more equally than heterosexual couples, the children have healthy peer relationships, and are emotionally well-adjusted (Ball & Pea, 1998; Kenyon et al., 2003). In the initial study of ten successful cases of second-parent adoption by Connolly (1998), the judges involved relied more on studies, and concluded "that there were no documented differences between children raised in homes of gays and lesbians and those raised in heterosexual homes" (p. 231). As Connolly pointed out then and in a more recent study (2002), the successful partners were subject to far more stringent examination of their living conditions, income, and parenting roles than is true for heterosexuals seeking parent status in the case of remarriage. A more recent study by Johnson and O'Connor (2002), involving 326 lesbian mothers and seventy-nine gay fathers (representing a total of 256 families) from thirty-four states and the District of Columbia found that their children's psychological adjustment, on a variety of levels, did not differ significantly from that of children raised by heterosexual parents. A smaller study, focused on adolescents being raised by same-sex female couples, similarly found that their psychological adjustment and school outcomes (GPA, trouble in school, and school connectedness), as well as their dating and romantic behaviors were similar to those of their peers being raised by heterosexual couples (Wainright, Russell, & Patterson, 2004). Given the results of these and other studies that show support for same-sex parenting, one has to question the effects on children who would not have this opportunity for adoption and thus would have to continue in foster care (Strasser, 2004).

Tye (2003) cited several studies, including those by the American Academy of Pediatrics (AAP) (2002a, 2002b) that supported the child-rearing practices of nonheterosexual parents and questioned the validity of the few studies that pointed to negative outcomes, in part because of the orientation of the researchers. These findings contradict assertions by Wardle (1997, 2004), who is regarded as perhaps the foremost opponent of adoption by homosexuals. He claims that this would be against the children's welfare, would subject them to rejection by peers and others, and have other negative effects. Karst (2003) alleges that Wardle's views are based largely on anecdotal reports rather than any scientific study. This agrees with the AAP's (2002a,b) view about perspectives of those doing research, the nature and size of the samples they use, and the wording of the questions they ask.

A survey of more than 300 private and public adoption agencies across the country with regard to adoption by lesbians and gays (Brodzinsky, 2003), moreover, found that more and more agencies are willing to place children with homosexual adults, which leads to more gay and lesbian adults becoming adoptive parents. Apparently, the agencies most likely to make such placements are "public, secular private, Jewish- and Lutheran-affiliated agencies, and those focusing on special needs and international adoption" (p. 3). For some agencies, especially those focusing on special needs children, homosexuals may be lower on the priority list for placements, meaning that perhaps the only children made available to them for adoption are those with special needs. Having such a hierarchy or priority list is not an uncommon practice among placement agencies, even for foster care, although 33.6 percent of the agencies in this study reported that they had a nondiscrimination policy (p. 4).

Lofton v. Kearney

The question of whether homosexuals can adopt was probably brought to public attention most forcefully in the case of *Lofton v. Kearney* (2001). In Florida, a boy who had been in the foster care of a homosexual for *nine years* was to be removed from that home to be placed for adoption (Cunningham, 2002). In what ways was this in his best interests? This restriction on the right of his homosexual foster father, a violation of principles stated by the American Law Institute (2002), did not appear to serve the child's best interests. Indeed, Cooper (2004), echoed the question raised by many professionals, if homosexuals are deemed "unfit" to be a child's legal parents, why are they considered "fit" to be foster parents, sometimes, as in Lofton's case, for several years for the same child?

To put this case into perspective, Steven Lofton and his partner, Roger Croteau, have served as foster parents for three children who were all HIV positive at birth; two of them subsequently suffered from AIDS. One boy, who was born with drugs in his system, is now drug free and no longer tested positive for HIV. Four other foster children are in the family. The children, four boys and a girl, range in age from early school age to adolescence. Lofton and Croteau are both registered nurses, and have cared for some of these children for more than ten years. The Children's Home Society in Florida created the "Lofton-Croteau" award to honor outstanding foster parents, and the two men were its first recipients. The children call them "Dad" and "Rodge" and regard one another as siblings.

When the boy, Bert (called John Doe in the suit), who had HIV was placed for adoption because he no longer tested positive for HIV, Lofton filed an application to adopt him. However, a Florida statute (63.042[3]—1995), enacted in 1977, categorically bans all homosexuals from adopting children. Lofton and other gay parents brought a class-action suit in 1999 seeking standing to adopt (under the Fourteenth Amendment—"equal protection"). The U.S. District Court, while acknowledging the strong bonds of attachment between the boy and Lofton, did not find that they warranted "extending the fundamental rights of family privacy, intimate association and family integrity" to these families. Nor did the court find that they had a fundamental right to adopt, be adopted, or apply for adoption. Thus, said the court, "the homosexual adoption provision does not tread upon any of the plaintiffs' asserted fundamental rights" (*Lofton v. Kearney*, 2001, at 1381). Rather, the court said that Bert's removal reflected the state's moral disapproval of homosexuality and its view that the best interests of children in the state would be served by being raised in a family that had both a mother and a father (Hong, 2003).

Lofton and the others involved filed an appeal, asserting, among other things, that

> not only was there a reasonable expectation of continuity, but that Florida created that expectation to begin with. Florida had repeatedly assured the Loftons that it would allow them to keep Doe as long as possible and did not recruit other adoptive parents so that Doe could stay with them. (Kim, 2003, p. 405)

Furthermore, Lofton et al. pointed out that (1) very few people in Florida were willing to adopt these HIV-positive children, and (2) that the state's *actions* showed that it didn't really believe that gays were harmful to children, since it placed children in foster care with gay parents, sometimes long term (as in the Lofton case), and with minimal, if any, state supervision.

On August 30, 2003, a federal judge ruled that Florida's law banning homosexuals adopting children was valid. At some point prior to this, Lofton and Croteau and their three foster children had apparently moved to Oregon (Cohen, 2003), although they are evidently still subject to Florida's laws regarding foster care. On January 28, 2004, the men lost an appeal in the Eleventh U. S. Circuit Court of Appeals, ruled on by a three-judge panel ("Around the nation," 2004). The full circuit court bench affirmed that verdict in July 2004, declining to rehear the case by a 6-6 vote.

In October 2004, the American Civil Liberties Union (ACLU) filed an appeal to the U.S. Supreme Court in this case. The question posed by the ACLU asked: "Did the Eleventh Circuit correctly hold that the Fourteenth Amendment permits a state categorically to exclude gay people and no one else from its case-by-case evaluation process for deciding who may adopt children into permanent homes?" (American Civil Liberties Union, 2004). On January 10, 2005, the Court announced, without comment, its refusal to hear the appeal (Associated Press, 2005a; Greenhouse, 2005; Henderson, 2005). That rejection of the ACLU appeal is "good" in the eyes of those who disapprove of homosexuals being able to adopt; it is "bad" in the eyes of those who may be torn from the only home they have ever known, as well as in the eyes of those who question the logic of Florida's law in this area.

INCOMPATIBILITY OF CHILD AND ADOPTIVE PARENTS

Sometimes, the child and the adoptive parents simply do not "fit." Perhaps the prospective parents were not given full information about the child's needs and prior experiences, or they were not given adequate postplacement support so that they were overwhelmed. They may not have anticipated the depth of the child's difficulties, or how many special needs the child has. These problems are exacerbated both by lack of information about where to go for needed services and by the cost of such services (Festinger, 2002). On the other hand, the placement agency may not have evaluated them appropriately, or sought full information. Either of these situations, or a combination of them, could make it difficult for a child and would-be parents to develop a familial relationship.

Given the extended period that some children spend in foster care prior to placement for adoption, or the number of foster homes in which they have been placed, a real potential exists for the child to have difficulty adjusting and developing an attachment to yet another set of adults. This may lead to acting-out behavior, testing the adoptive parents as it were, or to outright rejection of the caretaking adults. If the "testing" continues for an extended period, the parents may decide that they cannot go through with the adoption (Schwartz, 2000b). They may feel that it is their fault, that they do not have enough of whatever quality the youngster needs, or the youngster may have his or her self-perception of being "no good" reinforced by movement to yet a different caretaker. Perhaps they seek help first from other family members, or trusted friends. Ideally, they would be offered support and counseling by the agency that placed the child with them. The agency may supply one or more of the common post-permanency services such as "respite care (weekend or short-term to alleviate parental stress), camp and other summer activities, support groups for adoptive parents and children, educational support . . ., counseling, and assistance with finding and paying for residential treatment" (Testa, 2004, p. 125).

If these services fail, it is hoped that the parents seek a family therapist to try to resolve or reduce the difficulties before trying to dissolve the relationship legally. The public's attitude toward ending the relationship under such circumstances, according to a survey by Hollingsworth (2003), was more than two-to-one in favor of the parents being required to keep the child. This implies that those surveyed believed that "a family is a family," whether biological or adoptive in origin.

Difficulty in the adoptive parent-child relationship occurs in international as well as domestic adoptions. Here again there may be factors unknown to the adoptive parents: the mother's drug use, fetal alcohol syndrome, physical abuse of the mother while pregnant, malnutrition, neglect of the baby at home or in an orphanage, or other negative events. In addition, obviously, there is the transition for the child to a new environment and a foreign language. Thus, more difficulties may occur for the new family in the first year (Judge, 2003). If the child seems developmentally delayed at the initial evaluation, and again at an evaluation a few months later, more special needs may be present than anticipated initially. In any case, they may need more support from knowledgeable professionals in the first year than is usually available. Without such support, the parents may simply feel overwhelmed.

> If a decision is reached to terminate the placement, it must be done in such a way that the dignity and integrity of all concerned are maintained. Counseling will enable the child, the adoptive parents, and family members to gain insight into the precipitating factors, value mementos and memories of their lives together, and say goodbye. (Winkler, Brown, van Keppel, & Blanchard, 1988, p. 105)

SUMMARY

In this chapter, in contrast to the previous one, the focus of who or what causes adoption disruption is not on the biological parents, but rather is on the very people who are supposed to be most helpful in placement and support of the children and those who seek to care for them as adoptive parents. Whether the problem is provision of misinformation or too little information, or overloaded and possibly undertrained caseworkers, the end result is that the prospective adoptive families too often become "losers." In some cases, these social services problems may contribute to a child and would-be foster or adoptive parents finding that they are incompatible.

The Adoptive and Safe Families Act, while well-intentioned in its initiation, may be too rigid in its final format and practice to be beneficial to the children involved and their families, whether biological or adoptive. Other legislation, in some states, bans adoption by homosexuals or same-sex partners. As shown in *Lofton v. Kearny,* logical reasoning seems to be missing in permitting homosexuals to serve as foster parents. They often serve in that role for children with the most severe problems, but are not always permitted to adopt those children or others.

The factors discussed in this chapter represent only some of the causes of adoption disruption. Other examples are examined in the chapter to follow.

Chapter 4

Lives Disrupted

As difficult as preadoption disruptions may be, those that occur after the adoption has been finalized obviously bring at least equal anxiety and grief, and even more legal complications. One factor here, of course, is simply that the child in question tends to be older when the legal conflicts erupt and therefore at greater risk for emotional trauma when a separation is mandated. A second factor is that the attachment between the child and adoptive parents has had more years to develop, making the separation harder for all concerned.

Several cases of postadoption disruption were brought to national attention by the media in the past ten to fifteen years. One of the most "notorious," one might call it, was that of Baby Richard. This case shared the television screens with Baby Jessica's case, previously discussed, in the early 1990s. Also notorious is the case of the four Jackson boys, grossly undernourished and undersized, which emerged in late 2003 and that is still in the courts. A few cases, however, were worked out truly in the "best interests of the child," such as Baby Emily's case and that of a Choctaw Indian child adopted by nonmembers of the tribe. Although the causes for belated disruption in some cases parallel those of preadoption disruption—usually change of mind by a biological parent—the complications seem to be greater, as do the aftereffects.

ADOPTIONS DISSOLVED

The "Baby Richard" Case

Baby Richard was born in Illinois on March 16, 1991, to Daniella Janikova. She was then estranged from Richard's biological father,

When Adoptions Go Wrong
© 2006 by The Haworth Press, Inc. All rights reserved.
doi:10.1300/5780_04

Otokar ("Otto") Kirchner, and was living at a women's shelter when she decided to place her baby for adoption (Resnik, 1996). She executed her consent to adoption when the baby was four days old, and had told Otto's uncle to tell Otto that the baby had died shortly after birth. The prospective adoptive parents, the Does, filed a petition for adoption on March 20 and took Richard home as their son on that day. Less than two months later, Daniella reconciled with Otto and told him she had put their baby up for adoption. He quickly sought a lawyer, proved his paternity of the child, and sued to void the adoption proceedings since he had never terminated his parental rights to the boy. He lost at the trial-court level, and the Does were granted the adoption by this court in May 1992 (Resnik, 1996). Otto appealed to the Illinois Appellate Court, which ruled in the Does' favor as the adoption was found to be in the child's "best interests" (*In re* the petition of Doe, 1993).

Otto appealed next to the Illinois Supreme Court, which found that he had "full legal claim to Richard, overriding any claims of the boy or of the Does" [adoptive parents] (Denniston, 1995). Lowe (1996) reacted to the Illinois Supreme Court's characterization of Otto "again and again as the child's 'real' father who was entitled to 'preemptive rights' to a child he had never seen, let alone cared for" (p. 390). The Does had already formally adopted the boy and had raised him for almost four years. After the revocation by the Illinois court, appeals by the Does to the U.S. Supreme Court declined to hear the case.

> The Illinois Supreme Court's vacatur of Richard's adoption caused such a public outcry that the state legislature . . . enacted an amendment to the Adoption Act. The amendment provided that upon the vacation of an adoption proceeding a custody hearing was to take place in order to determine who should have custody of the child based upon the child's best interests. (Resnik, 1996, pp. 374-375)

This proviso, enacted on July 3, 1994, brought on a new round of court battles between Otto and the Does, again reaching the Illinois and U. S. Supreme Courts. The Illinois Supreme Court, having found a rationale on some unclear basis, and despite the passage of the new law, stated "State courts are not even to consider the child's interests in such a situation" (Denniston, 1995; see also *In re* Petition of Doe, 638 N.E. 2d 181, 182 [Ill. 1994], *cert. denied* 115 S. Ct. 499). The Illinois court ruled in Otto's favor on January 25, 1995, and ordered the Does to surrender the boy "forthwith." The U.S. Supreme Court denied a petition by the Does for a stay of that order. In her dissent to that ruling, Justice Sandra Day O'Connor wrote

> we can only speculate about the Illinois Supreme Court's rationale for avoiding application of a state law that mandates a "best interest" hearing. . . . I believe that in this case, "disrupting the *status quo* forthwith . . . has consequences whose disadvantages, from the point of view of the child's interests, outweigh any loss to the [biological father] that may result from a short delay in acquiring custody of the child." (*O'Connell v. Kirchner,* 1995)

Illinois' handling of the case certainly appears to perceive the child as a possession rather than a person. It also appears that the initial lies told by Daniella and others, compounded by Otto's lack of timely information and ignorance of Illinois law, should have been taken into consideration by the appellate court.

Richard, just past his fourth birthday when he was moved (April 30, 1995), was abruptly whisked away from the only family he had ever known, including a distraught and confused seven-year-old brother, and turned over to Otto and Daniella. The "surrender," as in Baby Jessica's case, was seen on television.[1] In the view of the attorneys for Richard's adoptive parents, the boy was treated like a piece of property, not as a human.

> Utterly ignoring Richard's rights, the court "ordered and directed [the adoptive parents] to surrender forthwith custody of the child known as Baby Boy Richard" and refused to order that the transfer of the child be supervised in any way by a professional who might help Richard deal with such an abrupt transition. (Bonina & Bahe-Jachna, 1999)

In late 2003, Baby Richard's psychologist, Karen Moriarty, published a book about the boy's experiences, which brings new information to light as well as an update on the Kirchners and others involved in this case (Moriarty, 2003). A number of important events are revealed in this book. First, apparently the Kirchners have reconciled, and have since had two daughters. Second, the adoptive parents, known as the "Does" during the custody battle, are identified as a couple named Robert (Jay) and Kimberly Warburton. Third, Richard, now known as Danny Kirchner, is, according to Dr. Moriarty, a healthy, bright, twelve-year-old boy with no emotional scars and only a few memories from his early childhood experience. Fourth, apparently Otto is still Danny's only legal custodial parent, as a judge refused to overturn Daniella's TPR document when she tried to regain legal status as Danny's mother in 1997. Moriarty spent two to three hours a day with Danny in his first year with the Kirchners, letting him do the talking and helping the parents as well, and subsequently visited the Kirchners a few times a week, gradually moving to phone conversations with Danny and his parents.[2] For a timetable of the "Baby Richard" case, see Exhibit 4.1.

The Maryland Family Code, as cited by Lowe (1996), has (or had) a list of eight factors to be considered in adoption and custody cases, with the focus clearly on the child's "best interests." The first two factors deal with the length of time the child has been with the prospective adoptive parents and the strength of the attachment to them; sincerity of the birth parents' desire to rear the child is factor number four; age of the child when he or she moved to the care of the prospective adoptive parents; and the two final items deal with abandonment by the child's father and his failure to support or visit the child (p. 394). That these factors might contribute to "exceptional circumstances" that would cause a court to rule one way or another is understandable. However, there is an additional assumption here that did not hold true in either the Baby Jessica case, discussed earlier, or in the Baby Richard case: everyone involved tells the truth to one another. In both of these cases, the mothers lied about, and to, the fathers, other relatives contributed to their lies, and even, if Boyer and Lubet (2000) and Moriarty (2003) are to be fully believed, some of the lawyers lied. Between the lies and deceptions on the one hand, and interminable court delays on the other, both Jessica and Richard would have remained with their adoptive parents under the Maryland code. Allowing deception and delay dictate the outcome is morally and ethically wrong.

The Gutierrez Case

A fifteen-year-old girl, Ashley Gutierrez, gave birth to a little girl in February 2002 in Amarillo, Texas, and gave her up for adoption.

EXHIBIT 4.1. Timetable in the "Baby Richard" Case

November 1989:	Daniella Janikova began living with Otokar ("Otto") Kirchner.
June 1990:	Daniella knew she was pregnant—both she and Otto looking forward to having their baby.
January 1991:	Otto returned to Czechoslovakia to see the grandmother who raised him before she died.
	Otto's aunt calls Daniella from Czechoslovakia to tell her that Otto is dating his ex-girlfriend while he is there.
February 1991:	Daniella moves out of the apartment she shares with Otto, moves to a women's shelter, where it is suggested that she might place her expected baby for adoption.
	Daniella meets the Does. She refuses to give the father's name to them.
March 16, 1991:	Daniella gives birth to a boy (at a hospital near the Does rather than the one at which Otto knew she was to deliver). She refuses Otto's calls, and ultimately has his uncle tell him that the baby died at birth.
March 19, 1991:	The Does take the baby from the hospital and file a petition to adopt him, falsely alleging that they have tried to locate the unknown father.
	Otto searches for a death certificate or other information about the baby and finds none.
May 12, 1991:	Daniella and Otto reunite and she tells him of the baby's birth and adoption (57 days). (*In re* the Petition of Doe, 627 N.E. 2d [Ill.App.Ct. 1993] at 650-651; Moriarty, 2003, p. 526, #3) False affidavits (Moriarty, 2003, p. 530]
June 6, 1991:	Otto's attorney appeared on his behalf in court.
May 8, 1992:	Otto's parental rights are terminated because he did not claim them within the statutory limit of 30 days postdelivery. [Moriarty, 2003, p. 531]
June 16, 1994:	Illinois Supreme Court unanimously (7-0) overturned the adoption. (*In re* Petition of Doe, 638 N.E. 2d [Ill. 1994])

(continued)

(continued)

July 3, 1994:	Illinois state legislature passed a law that mandated consideration of the best interests of the child, to be applied to all pending cases including the *Warburton vs. Kirchner* case.
November 7, 1994:	U.S. Supreme Court declines to take the case (cert. denied, 115 S.Ct. 499 [1994])
January 12, 1995:	Cook County District Court refused to dismiss a custody petition filed by the Warburtons (citing the new law passed in July 1994)
January 25, 1995:	Illinois Supreme Court orders the Does to turn the baby over to Otto Kirchner "forthwith."
January 1995 (late):	Warburtons appealed to U. S. Supreme Court.
February 13,1995:	U. S. Supreme Court denied the request for a hearing to issue a stay (5-2). (*O'Connell v. Kirchner,* 115 S.Ct. 1084 [1995])
March 28, 1995:	First meeting between Warburtons and Kirchners to arrange the transfer—allegedly much conflict and finger pointing.
April 30, 1995:	"Baby Richard" transferred to Otto and Daniella Kirchner.
July 1997:	Daniella seeks to have her consent to adoption vacated. This was denied.
	Warburtons file petition asserting that Daniella "intentionally inflicted severe emotional harm" on them.

Jeff and Alicia Gurney took the child home from the hospital and have cared for her since then. Five months later, her mother wanted her baby back, saying she did not want to give her up for adoption (Wilson, 2004a). Nevertheless, a jury terminated her rights and those of the biological father, Joseph Gonzales, in May 2003, a ruling that was reversed by an appeals court in January 2004. The reversal was based on the fact that neither parent had signed anything to terminate their parental rights.

In April, the Gurneys appealed that decision to the Texas Supreme Court, which denied a rehearing in August. At that time, Judge James

Anderson named the four biological and adoptive parents as "temporary joint management conservators" for preschooler Savannah Sierra Gutierrez (McBride, 2004). This allowed the child to remain with the Gurneys, but awarded Gutierrez and Gonzalez visitation rights pending a final custody hearing in November. The Gurneys shortly thereafter filed another lawsuit seeking temporary custody. That was denied by the county court on September 9, 2004 (Wilson, 2004a). Judge Anderson did, however, establish a visiting schedule for Gutierrez and Gonzalez that gradually increased the time they might spend with the child from the time of his ruling until December 2004.[3]

This arrangement did not last long. District Court Judge John Board ruled on September 20 that the schedule was in conflict with the ruling from the appeals court, despite a request from the Gurneys' attorney to let the transition format continue as planned (Wilson, 2004b). Although the girl was with her biological mother while Judge Board made this decision, apparently Ashley Gutierrez chose to return the child to the Gurneys as scheduled. Under the new court order, however, she would regain custody of her daughter at 6 p.m. on September 21. Alice Gurney told the child what was going to happen, and the child allegedly said that she did not want to go with Ashley.

Earlier in the day, Judge Board, addressing the Gurneys and Ashley Gutierrez, said that "The presumption is parents are going to act in the best interests of the child. . . . It's up to y'all to make that presumption the truth" (Wilson, 2004b). Joe Marr Wilson, attorney for the Gurneys, indicated that he would appeal, but had little expectation of success with that move. *"By the time an appeal is heard,* the child will have been with her biological parents for such a time the courts 'won't rip her back out'" (Wilson, 2004b; italics added). As with other cases included here, this one bears witness to the lengthy periods between the filing of an appeal and the hearing of it, and not necessarily for the ultimate benefit of the child. Indeed, it is almost as if each case reinforces the perception that children are seen more as property or possessions than as people.

Potential Dissolution for Cause

Four boys placed with Raymond and Vanessa Jackson first as foster children, and subsequently adopted, were, according to their "parents," subject to a condition that made them not eat. However, in October 2003, the oldest boy, Bruce, was detected seeking food in a neighbor's garbage can in the middle of the night. He looked as if he was ten years old, not nineteen, and weighed less than fifty pounds. The other three boys were similarly undernourished and underdeveloped for their ages.[4] Within the first month after being placed in other homes, they had each gained weight and height, and were eating quite normally, without ill effects. Four months later, Bruce had gained more than thirty pounds and grown six inches. The younger boys had made similar progress (Shiffman, Lipka, & Graham, 2004). One year later, Bruce had gained 100 pounds and had grown a foot taller, and his younger brothers were similarly gaining and growing.

In May 2004, the grand jury in their New Jersey county issued a twenty-eight-count indictment that included several charges of chronic endangerment and aggravated assault. Apart from malnutrition, they had not received medical or dental care in years. That these adoptions should be dissolved as a life-saving measure seemed self-evident. Raymond and Vanessa Jackson entered pleas of "not guilty" in court on July 12, 2004 (Graham & Shiffman, 2004). At a court hearing on September 20, 2004, an eating disorders expert reviewing the boys' medical files for the defense was given until December 6 to complete that task (Shiffman, 2004).

The role of the social workers in this case was apparently poorly carried out, possibly because of case overload and/or inadequate attention to required inspections. Furthermore, apparently unlike law, psychology, and other professions, not all social workers are required to attend regular, continuing education (Kay, 2002). (No charges had been made public against the social workers involved at the time this was being written, although their actions were being investigated, and little information was available on the workers who had been involved at one time or another with the Jacksons.) New Jersey had assigned one social worker to the boys and their foster families, a considerable difference from the earlier state of affairs.

One year after Bruce Jackson was found digging in his neighbor's garbage, the boys were all thriving, having doubled their weight and grown several inches (Lipka, Shiffman, & Graham, 2004). According to an emeritus professor of pediatrics cited in this article, Robert Blizzard, the boys had suffered from "psychosocial dwarfism," a syndrome in which the growth hormones of children emotionally deprived and psychologically abused effectively shut down—"stunting their height, preventing puberty, even retarding their intelligence" (Lipka, Shiffman, & Graham, 2004, p. B5). An interview with Raymond and Vanessa Jackson contradicted this. The Jacksons asserted that earlier chaos in the boys' lives resulted in the boys overeating regular food (as well as nonnutritional and nonedible items), followed by throwing up—a form of bulimia, as it were (France, 2004). The media also reported, on November 15, 2004, that Raymond Jackson had been admitted to the hospital after suffering a stroke. He died on November 30. The court hearing, scheduled for early December, was postponed. A brief hearing on January 18, 2005, included: the prosecution's motion to dismiss charges against Raymond Jackson, Vanessa Jackson's attorney announcing plans to have a psychiatrist and a pediatrician examine the four boys, and the scheduling for another hearing on March 17 (Graham, 2005a). In November 2005, Vanessa Jackson pleaded guilty to one charge of child endangerment, for which she could receive a sentence of seven years in prison, with release possible much earlier (Graham, 2005b). This was, indeed, the sentence she received early in 2006 (Graham, 2006). Bruce presented a statement at Vanessa Jackson's sentencing in February 2006, with video statements also being offered by his three younger brothers. He indicated that, as she had taken away his childhood, she should be sentenced to life in prison. Obviously, this did not happen.

Bruce Jackson has grown more than a foot and gained about 100 pounds since being found in October 2003, but is living "under constant supervision in a state-run home and suffers lingering physical deficits and emotional trauma" (Graham & Shiffman, 2006). Two of his younger brothers have been adopted and the third boy's adoption is pending. New Jersey's Division of Youth and Family Services, in March 2005, purportedly offered the four boys $10 million to settle the case, but their lawyers had not responded to the offer by early April (Mulvihill, 2005). In November 2005, the state confirmed an agreement to pay $12.5 million to settle a civil suit filed on behalf of the brothers (Graham, 2005c).

A similar case came to light in early February 2005 involving John and Linda Dollar of Florida, who were captured in Utah as fugitives from Florida on warrants of felony aggravated child abuse (Associated Press, 2005b). The Dollars were adoptive parents of eight children, seven of them aged twelve to seventeen. Their abuse was discovered when one of the children (or Linda Dollar) called for an ambulance for the sixteen-year-old boy who had been seriously injured. Five of the children "told investigators that they were tortured by the couple, subjected to electric shocks, beatings with hammers and having their toenails yanked out with pliers" (Associated Press, 2005b, p. 14). They were all malnourished. Like the Jackson boys, they were seriously underweight and undersized for their ages. All were being homeschooled, and they were rarely seen outside by neighbors. The other two children were apparently favored by the Dollars and did not show the same signs of abuse. All seven children were placed in the custody of the Department of Children and Families. The eighth child, age twenty, no longer lived with the family (Vansickle & Krueger, 2005).

The Dollars apparently moved frequently—from Tennessee to Florida and back again, as well as within the state of Florida. They had adopted children in both states, and there had been no complaints to state welfare agencies. Whether the adoptions will now be dissolved remains to be seen (Vansickle & Krueger, 2005). In September 2005, the Dollars made a plea agreement that would place each of them in prison for fifteen years followed by fifteen years' probation, but would avert prosecution in other jurisdictions. It is interesting to note that the agreement "came less than a week after prosecutors released testimony from a psychologist who likened the children's treatment to that of prisoners of war" (Tunstall, 2005).

In yet a third case, a couple in Ohio were accused of forcing some of their adopted, special needs children to live in chages. Michael and Sharen Gravelle had adopted eleven children, ages one to fifteen years, who were reported to have pshychological and behavioral problems stemming from fetal alcohol syndrome, and a condition that involved eating nonfood items (shades of the Jackson case!) (AP, 2006; Sheeran, 2006). Adult children of the couple testified, at a hearing to transfer custody of the children to the state, that their father and stepmother not only had provided little food for them, but had even charged them rent to live in the family home. Furthermore, the Gravelles had a hired a private social worker to work with the children, but she had never reported the child abuse or endangerment. A county social worker discovered the caged children in September 2005, which resulted in their being placed in foster homes (Sheeran, 2006).

ON THE POSITIVE SIDE

As mentioned earlier, several statutes were enacted in the past two decades to hasten permanent placement of children, but the U.S. Indian Child Welfare Act of 1978 was exempt from many of the provisions. This law was an effort to maintain tribal integrity and coherence in the face of a number of challenging problems. The Act obviously affected adoption within and outside of the tribes.

The Choctaw Indian Twins

"Roy" and "Thelma," twins, were born in December 1985 to a couple who were members of the Choctaw tribe of Mississippi but living off the reservation. They were placed with a non-Indian couple—the Holyfields—for adoption (Goldstein & Goldstein, 1996). The adoption was legalized in January 1986. Two months later, the tribe tried to upset the adoption, but this was rejected by the Mississippi state court in July 1986. The latter ruling was affirmed by the Mississippi Supreme Court in 1987, and then the decision was appealed to the U.S. Supreme Court (*Mississippi Band,* 1988).

In April 1989, when the twins were more than three years old, the U.S. Supreme Court ruled that the Mississippi Supreme Court was wrong—the case should have been heard by a tribal court. Justice Brennan commented, "It is not ours to say whether the trauma that might result from removing these children from their adoptive family should outweigh the interest of the Tribe" (Goldstein & Goldstein, 1996, p. 49).

Ultimately, the case was heard by the Choctaw Tribal Court which, in February 1990 (when the twins were four years old), ruled that they should remain with their mother. "The decision . . . respected the twins' need for continuity of care and allowed them to remain with their adoptive mother who had become their psychological parent" (Goldstein & Goldstein, 1996, p. 54). This decision also considered the trauma already experienced by the children when their adoptive father died during the time of the litigation.

Baby Emily

The "Baby Emily" case involved an unmarried father refusing to relinquish his parental rights, as seen in cases previously discussed, but had a different outcome. Baby Emily was given up for adoption at age three days (born August 28, 1992), and adopted by Stephen and Angel Welsh in Florida. Her biological father had not waived his rights to consent to the adoption, although allegedly when Emily's mother said in June 1992 that she was considering adoption, he told her to "do whatever you have to do" (Rosenman, 1995, p. 1861). The next month he told the mother's attorney that he would not consent to the adoption.

The trial court, which first found in the father's favor in October 1992, reheard the case just over a year later, and reversed the prior judgment as it found that the father had abandoned the mother during the last three months of her pregnancy. The reversal was based on a provision in Florida law that the court could consider the behavior of the father toward the mother during her pregnancy. Emily's birth mother was ready to rescind her consent for the adoption in order to prevent the father from gaining custody because of his neglect and cruelty to her. This ruling was reversed by the appeals court, but was later upheld by the Supreme Court of Florida in July 1995, which stated "a trial court, in making a determination of abandonment, may consider the lack of emotional support and/or emotional abuse by the father of the mother during her pregnancy" (Resnik, 1996, p. 377). Emily was two years old when the courts reversed the adoption. It was then again reversed in July 1995, by which time Emily was almost three years old. Her biological father was apparently going to try to take his case to the U.S. Supreme Court, but in January 1996, the Court refused to hear the biological father's appeal of that decision (Hansen, 1996). (A thorough search of the available information on the Internet and in Lexis-Nexis provided no later information on the Baby Emily case.)

SUMMARY

The cases just discussed have in common only one factor: the adoption of the children involved had already been finalized in the courts. Other than that, however, the situations are quite different. Two cases were resolved in a positive way, with the deciding authorities arguing or recognizing the need for stability in a child's life despite strong positive claims to move the child, whether to a biological parent or to a tribe.

In the Jackson case, the foster/adoptive parents clearly had some unique perspectives with regard to the four boys. This was quite different from that which governed their behavior toward their biological children *and* their adopted daughters. The Jacksons were being paid first as foster parents of the boys and later as their adoptive parents with state subsidies (Lipka, Sheffman, & Graham, 2004). That no agency worker questioned any of this is irresponsible and unprofessional, not to mention possibly criminal. Indeed, all of New Jersey's social welfare services came under heavy scrutiny recently as a result of this case, and a few others. What was supposed to have been done as routine follow-up was not done, with tragic results.

The situation with the Dollars and the Gravelles, similar in some ways to that of the Jacksons, raises many questions about their motives for abusing so many of their adopted children, and also why the abuses were never reported. Ways to prevent such tragedies are presented in a later chapter.

Chapter 5

Effects of the Disruption

A brief resynthesis of the material presented to this point will facilitate a discussion of the effects of a disrupted adoption. Some adoptions are made independently, either directly or through an intermediary, and others are the result of placement by an adoption or other social services agency. The adoptive parents may or may not have had appropriate legal advice concerning termination of parental rights and other potential difficulties en route to a successful adoption. As can be seen in the cases presented, differences in state laws and their interpretation contribute substantially to the disruptions in adoption.

If you live with someone, or someone lives with you, for a week, a month, a year or more, some kind of relationship develops. If it is positive, a strong and special attachment may even develop. If this is disrupted, in most cases (except, perhaps, for very young infants), all parties involved will feel distress at some level.

TIME FOR THERAPY

A disrupted adoption is very much like the death of a child. The loss is the same for the parents, as the child they have come to love is gone; the grief is often the same. The ability to discuss the loss with others, even in the family, may be very difficult, as not everyone recognizes the depth of psychological bonds even in the absence of biological ones. The adoptive parents may seek grief therapy, even just for a few sessions, simply to help them regain their composure enough to continue parenting any other children they may have, as well as to face their jobs and other aspects of their daily lives. If their therapist or caseworker knows of a support group for adoptive parents

When Adoptions Go Wrong
© 2006 by The Haworth Press, Inc. All rights reserved.
doi:10.1300/5780_05

who have lost a child, especially through disruption or dissolution, they might refer the bereaved parents to that group.

Similarly, the child, if nursery-school age or older, might be helped with the abrupt transition through play therapy if quite young, or other psychotherapy techniques if older. Replacing existing bonds of attachment is quite a challenge for anyone, but especially for a child. Rarely is there an "automatic," let alone immediate, change of allegiance from the adoptive family to the biological parent(s) solely on the grounds of genetic connection.

It would be very difficult to design a clinical protocol that would benefit all of those who find themselves in this painful situation. There are so many factors to consider, some individual, some familial, and some legal. How old is the child? How long has the child been with the family? Are the bereft adoptive parents individuals who "fall apart" when struck by negative events, or are they resilient enough to pick themselves up, as it were, and move forward, even with pain in their hearts? Is there concern between the parents and for their other child(ren), if any? Are they planning to fight the disruption in court? Do they have a realistic view of what a legal battle entails in their state? Do they have the stamina for a protracted legal battle (as so many of these suits are)? Can they find a therapist who understands their situation?

RESTATEMENT OF CAUSES

Changes of mind on the part of the biological mothers for one reason or another, are obviously one source of the disruption problem. Some pregnancies result from casual relationships with men who first disappeared from the mother's life for one reason or another, and then reappeared to oppose termination of their parental rights whether because they truly wanted to parent the child or because they wanted to make trouble for the child's mother, or, in some cases, expect or hope that the would-be adoptive parents might be willing to give him money (a "pay off" as it were), to disappear forever.

Another potential cause of disruption may arise when a child is removed from the biological parent(s) because of substance abuse, placed in foster care, and ultimately adopted with the parental rights terminated by court order rather than voluntarily. There may or may not be direct contact between the biological parent(s), the child, and the adoptive parent thereafter, but there may well be appeals to the court to overturn an adoption. As was seen in a case in Michigan, the case dragged on and on, although ultimately the mother gave up her effort to regain custody of her six-year-old son (Anonymous, 2004b).

Legal obstacles have also caused disruptions of one kind or another. In *Lofton v. Kearney,* as in others involving homosexuals who wish to adopt, there is a need to recognize that gay and lesbian couples, or individuals, have been recognized as highly capable caretakers of children. In many situations, their relationships have been longerlasting and more harmonious than those of married heterosexuals, yet they may not be allowed to adopt children who need a permanent home, even when those children have lived with the would-be adoptive parents as foster children, perhaps for many years.

> Undoubtedly, some lawmakers believe that it is always bad for a child to be raised by people who are homosexual, so much so that even children who are in foster care and who will have no other opportunity for adoption would be better off remaining in foster care. But the evidence of how children turn out after being raised by homosexual parents does not support such an absolutist position, even on its own terms. Most children raised by homosexual parents become happy, healthy adults who are good citizens and who are very thankful that they did not spend their entire youth bouncing around in foster care. (Dwyer, 2003, p. 892)

Vermont has recognized same-sex relationships with a ceremony celebrating their "civil union" (Markowitz, 2005) and Massachusetts permits actual marriage (*Goodenough v. Mass. Dept. of Public Health,* 2003), yet other states place statutory obstacles in the path of finding good permanent homes for children who therefore remain in the foster care system. Even in states that permit adoption by homosexual individuals or couples, local judges may find a way to dismiss their adoption petitions (Brodzinksy, 2003). These barriers stem from homophobic attitudes that may have religious roots, or stereotypes and misconceptions that perceive homosexuals as emotionally disturbed, possibly sexually abusive, and ill equipped to function as parents. The evidence from a number of studies strongly suggests that these biases are baseless (Brodzinsky, 2003).

A VARIETY OF EFFECTS

Effects on the Child

If one looks at children in families in which the parents have separated en route to divorce, their anxiety and distress are patently obvious. Consider then how much greater their bewilderment would be if one of those parents moved out of the child's life completely. In such situations, most parents would seek counseling for the child to enable the youngster to understand and cope with the problem rather than become withdrawn, highly anxious, or acting out in negative ways. If a custody dispute is involved, the court generally orders a psychological study in an effort to determine the contest's outcome. In some jurisdictions, the child even has an advocate or a guardian-ad-litem to represent the child's needs and/or wishes.

In adoption disruption, however, a different pattern is found. There is little question that the abrupt transfer of a child from the only family he or she knows to utter strangers is even more traumatic than the separation in parental custody fights, especially if the child is older than five or six months. The abrupt transfer is one factor that could be altered. Representation of the child is imperative here, and, perhaps even to a greater degree than in divorce-based custody conflicts, and yet it rarely occurs. As to therapy, there is no indication that this is even ordered by the court, let alone considered by the biological parent(s). Moriarty's role with the Kirchners and Baby Richard appears to be an exception to this pattern (Moriarty, 2003).

Assuming normal development, movement from one caretaker or family to another before the infant is six months old should result in comparatively less emotional damage for the child. By six months of age, however, and certainly within a month or two after that, the baby has formed bonds of attachment to his or her caretaker(s) and would be less likely to form new bonds easily with the new one(s) (Erikson, 1950; Weiner & Elkind, 1978). The so-called "Internet Twins" would certainly have difficulty becoming emotionally attached to anyone as the result of being moved several times before they were even one year old, and might well cling to each other as the only constant figures in their young lives.

Not only are there bonds of attachment between child and caretakers, based on love rather than blood, but a child begins to have a sense of identity, a key element of which is the child's name. What was the effect on Baby Jessica who became Anna, Baby Richard who became Danny, Savannah Gutierrez who became Sierra, and Evan Scott who became Evan Johnson? Confusion could be one result, at least initially. In what ways did the new, if biological, parents explain the name change to the child? Did the child feel as if his or her "original" persona was "bad?" Even Moriarty's detailed account of the Baby Richard case (Moriarty, 2003) did not mention this element of the transfer.[1]

By the time a child is eighteen months old, and until he or she is about five or six years old, when disruption occurs in the family, whether via parental divorce or upset of an adoption, the child tends to assume the blame for the dissolved relationship. During the primary school years and perhaps into the preteens, the child may be confused as to where he or she belongs, who is "family" and who is not, and whether it is "safe" to develop an emotional tie to anyone. As Barth and Berry (1988) state,

> Older adopted children are not open packages of sculptor's clay willing to be formed into the image of the adopting parents. The effects of the child's prior experience in birth and foster families affects current expectations and cognitive and behavioral responses to stress. (p. 48)

Should the adoption disruption occur in adolescence, the teenager may simply become rebellious and defiant, or withdraw from interaction with those in the household. Although there are such "typical" reactions, remember that each child's response is unique in that it is based on specific circumstances interacting with individual characteristics. This can lead to a variety of clinical problems:

- Disrupted attachment and/or feelings of disconnectedness
- Splitting of good/bad self
- Damaged self-image, low self-esteem
- Feelings of rejection
- Feelings of shame and guilt
- Problems in identity development
- Perceived lack of control
- Feelings of loss and unresolved grief
- Active fantasy life
- Learning disabilities

In one study, limited though it is in number of participants, insight is gained into the reactions of three adolescents who had been in foster care and adoptive homes for most of their young lives (Bowman, 1995). By age fourteen, they had collectively been in thirty-four different homes. They each said they had difficulty developing a sense of self, of identity. They were usually *not* told why they were being moved from one caretaking family to another, even when they had been with the family for many months or even a few years; and they were justifiably (in this author's mind) angry and suffering with feelings of abandonment. This frequency of placements and replacements may be unusually high, but multiple placements *do* occur and are rarely in the child's "best interests." At the very least, as these youths reported, they affect a child's ability to develop attachments to new caretakers. Apart from raising the question of "Who do you trust?," they might well think, "Why bother? I'll only be yanked away again in a few weeks or months."

"When parents adopt an older child with an extensive history of early trauma and loss, it often takes great effort and an even longer time to establish a trusting relationship" (Shapiro, Shapiro, & Paret, 2001a, p. 70). As Bowman's (1995) interviewees indicated, such children have difficulty trusting any adults, which may be reflected in their keeping an emotional distance from the adoptive parents, acting out in school, depression, and developmental regression. If the adoptive parents are overwhelmed by such behaviors, and have little or no support from counselors or social workers, they may painfully decide to give up the effort, which would lead to yet another transfer.

Effects on Other Children in the Family

How do you explain to a seven-year-old, let alone a three-year-old, why the sibling who was there when the older child went to sleep the night before was not there the next morning? Or was being taken away by somebody never seen before?

If there are other children in the family, biological or not, the removal of one child affects them all. Older children, if adopted, may well ask themselves, "Is my mother going to come for me?" or, conversely, "Why doesn't my mommy want *me* back?" Even biological children in the family may question, "Could I be taken away from my mom and dad?" At minimum, they will experience a loss, possibly traumatic. In the Baby Richard case, for example, a seven-year-old brother looked utterly bewildered and upset as Richard was driven away and who, a year later, had not seen him again (Schwartz, 2000a). Indeed, after an NBC *Dateline* presentation on the Baby Richard case, the author wrote to the network, "consideration should also be given to the effects of any removal of Richard from his present home on the older child of the adoptive parents. He is not old enough to comprehend the nuances of this painful situation and may well need supportive therapy to see him through this traumatic experience"[2] (Author's files, July 28, 1994). The effects on the other children in the family will vary with their age, but even a toddler will be aware that someone is missing, will ask questions, and may exhibit behavioral signs of distress.

Questions about what happened to the "disappeared" sibling may well persist well into adulthood. One young man, by then in his early thirties, asked his adoptive parents—out of the blue—about a little brother he recalled who had mysteriously "vanished" more than twenty-five years earlier (Author's case files). They explained, truthfully, that the biological mother had changed her mind and they felt they had had no choice but to return the younger child. If this situation had occurred many years later than it did, the parents might have considered going to court as others have done, but they also would and should have had to consider the impact of the legal battle not only on themselves, but on the remaining child as well. It would be an admittedly difficult decision to make.

In the situation where children are removed from a home and placed in foster care, siblings may not always be placed in the same foster home. With the time pressures set by ASFA, they may be moved into separate adoptive homes, with the real possibility that they lose touch with one another permanently (Groza, Mascmeier, Jamison, & Piccola, 2003). However, if a sincere effort is to be made to keep sibling ties intact, the planning for this must occur at the beginning of placement services. The benefits accruing to siblings kept together far outweigh the benefits attached to separating them, except, perhaps, if one of the siblings is abusive to another. Among other things, they feel safer in a new home when someone as familiar as a sibling is with them, and are thus better able to become attached to the new family. The children's wishes also need to be considered, as well as the availability of an adoptive family willing to adopt more than one child at a time.

Effects on the Adoptive Parents

Adoption disruption can stem from a number of sources. Most cases are due to conflicts over parental rights; some occur due to the adoptive parents' inability to cope with the children's problems, whatever they may be.

For most of the parents, in either event, disruption of the adoption they have undertaken with commitment is cataclysmic. As with losing a child to illness or accident, it is a kind of death. Whether they have gone through an extensive court battle, as was true in the Baby Richard, Baby Jessica, and Savannah Sierra Gutierrez cases, or been given only twenty-four hours' notice when the adoption has not been finalized, they have lost a child they have come to love. Jeff Gurney, would-be adoptive father of Savannah Gutierrez, said at the time of the adverse decision that he and his wife would be devastated if they lost her, although eventually they would be able to "move on." His concern for the child is that "she's the one who has to go into a whole new environment and frankly, not a very good environment. It's heartbreaking" (Wilson, 2004). Their attorney was quoted as saying, "Let's just pretend she died in a car wreck" (Wilson, 2004a). Scarnecchia (1994), citing a psychologist's view of the effects of such a loss on the adoptive parents, said that the effects include severe depression, rage at the unfairness of the law and social service systems, total helplessness, pain in knowing that the child is suffering in the changed situation, and loss of self-esteem.

Mourning the loss may be greater if this is the parents' only child; handling the mourning becomes more difficult if other children are in the home. Although they may show their grief, parents need also to reassure the other child(ren) of their love *and* security. The grief may ease over the years, as grief does under most circumstances, so that individuals can continue to function in their many roles, but the memory of the loss remains. It may be ameliorated to some degree by new adoptions (along with the rationalization that these later children would not have been theirs had the loss not occurred).

The grandparents of the child who is removed are usually also grief stricken, unless they were opposed to the idea of adoption altogether.

Even then, if they are caring parents, they will try to come to the emotional aid of *their* children. Apart from physically holding their children close, if they live anywhere near them, they can be good listeners. They can help with their remaining grandchildren while the saddened parents try to recover their equanimity.

In other situations, some of the special needs' adoptions have brought overwhelming problems with which the new family simply cannot manage, and for which they may not have been properly prepared. Barth and Berry (1988) discussed many of these cases, some of which have already been cited. One case, although in a slightly different context, was a transracial adoption. Would-be adoptive parents are certainly aware of racial differences to some degree, but, as several Canadians discovered to their sorrow, these obvious factors may not be the primary root of the children's problems (Adams, 2002).

Transracial Adoption in Canada

An examination of what a small sample of Canadian adoptive parents, five couples, experienced may illuminate the effects of disrupted adoption on most parents. To a considerable degree, official Canadian policy toward its native or aboriginal population for many years led to children being separated from their tribes yet not becoming part of the larger society. Indeed, besides residential placement away from the tribe, the government promoted the adoption of these children by white families. The adoptive parents "were confident and optimistic that they could provide a nurturing home environment for adopted children. . . . They believed in nurture over nature . . ." (Adams, 2002, p. 97), and that love and positive child-rearing techniques would overcome whatever problems the child might have from reservation life and earlier life experiences.

The children's feelings of lack of identity and low self-esteem were already present when they were taken into nonnative homes. They were not infants, which aggravated the problem somewhat. They had difficulty bonding with their adoptive families, with peer relationships, with school behavior, and other life aspects that were at odds with the "ideal family" expectations of the adoptive parents (Adams, 2002). When the youths either left home, or the "parents" asked social services to place them elsewhere, the parents were both relieved at the removal of turmoil from the family and devastated at their loss. Each of the couples interviewed had a sense of personal failure and guilt at being unable to get their adopted son off of a self-destructive track. Initially, they denied the boy's problems. When they finally had to face those problems, the parents felt frustration accompanied by an anger that they could barely admit feeling, even to themselves. They were concerned about the impact of the son's behavior on everyone in the family, and also frustrated by the lack of support on the part of the social service agency which seemed to blame all of the boy's problems on the parents. Adams also found interesting gender differences:

> The mothers spoke more often than the fathers did about the change in the way they evaluated their parenting abilities. . . . The childrearing practices they had learned and had successfully used on their other children were not effective, and they lost confidence in themselves and became emotionally distraught. . . .What the fathers spoke of was their frustration with two elements of the situation: one, they were not able to control their son, even though they had tried everything; and, two, they had difficulty with their wives' reactions and obsessiveness, their excessive crying and talking. (2002, pp. 114-115)

In each of the families in the sample, the son's behavior that led to these feelings was so opposite to what the parents had earlier observed, and obviously expected to continue, that the son became a "stranger" or an "imposter" in their eyes. For all their caring, the son rejected them and their affection and values. The parents then moved through the emotional stages to grief—grief at the loss of the son they thought they had, and grief at the pain caused to other members of the family. All of them sought help from legal and social welfare sources, and apparently in each case those sources perceived the *parents* as the cause of the boy's problems.

Only when the parents were able to learn more about the children's lives *before* their adoption could they begin to heal. This information typically was *not* given to the prospective parents, as may also happen in international adoptions. The withholding of pertinent life information by the agencies or individual intermediaries involved is the basis for what is called a "wrongful adoption," discussed earlier in Chapter 3. Had the appropriate information been provided, there might have been a somewhat more positive outcome. Approximately 95 percent of the adoptions of native children by nonnative parents failed (Adams, 2002). Although genetic factors may have contributed to the children's problems, there were additional factors: fetal alcohol syndrome, which was apparently a common problem among the native Canadians, as was postnatal abuse at the residential schools and elsewhere; negative stereotyping of the First Nations (native) people; and neglect of natives' welfare at all levels (Adams, 2002). Support groups did help some of the parents in the aftermath of their loss.

SUMMARY

For most parents in adoption disruption cases, the pattern is the same in terms of frustration and anger, as well as grief experienced and ultimately handled. In cases in which the adoptive parents request the removal of the child, they also have to deal with initial denial of the problem, whatever its source may be, and feelings of their own guilt and failure. Much more is needed for them in terms of pre-adoption information *and* postplacement/adoption support.

Many, perhaps most, adoptive parents figuratively hold their breath until a child's final adoption papers are signed by a judge. Having heard stories of children being removed before the papers were signed, or of prolonged court battles, they fear the same thing happening to them. If it does, they are typically grief stricken, perhaps bewildered, certainly distraught, just as if their child had died suddenly. Whether they wallow in their distress depends on their personalities and maybe even on their prior experiences of loss of a family member. In addition is the factor of other children in the family who need comfort for their pain, as well as the normal day-to-day care those children need from parents. They need help in facing their loss, and help in answering the questions of other family members and friends. Obviously, what they tell others depends on the nature and depth of their relationship, but they usually do have to respond in some way to painful questions for at least the first few months after the adoption is disrupted. As has been seen here, whatever the source of the separation, the pain and grief are similar.

SECTION II:
LEGAL ISSUES: PRECEDENTS
AND PREVENTION

Chapter 6

In Whose "Best Interests"?

"OPEN ADOPTION" AND DISRUPTION

Given the largely negative and painful outcomes of prolonged litigation in disputed custody cases, one has to wonder whether there might be alternatives that might truly be more in a child's "best interests." As noted earlier, some agencies and some biological parents insist that an adoption be "open" permitting ongoing "live" contact between those parents and the child they have permitted to be adopted. That is one option, obviously. Another is more limited to perhaps an annual photo of the child being sent to the birth mother, together with notes on the child's health, schooling, and interests. It would seem appropriate in any open adoption for the adult parties to renegotiate their relationship as the child grows and perhaps as his or her needs change.

Benefits and Difficulties

Clearly, there are benefits and difficulties related to open adoption, and there are not enough good longitudinal studies regarding outcomes of such relationships to offer firm guidance to the parties involved (Berry, 1993; Winkler et al., 1988). One recent study, however, does reflect the feelings of a sample of thirty adoptive parents seven years after they became involved in an open adoption (Siegel, 2003). Siegel asked her subjects several Likert-scaled questions regarding open adoption. Although the subjects were divided on several questions, they were unanimous in agreeing, "I worry about how open adoption may affect my child" (p. 413). Only two worried about the birth parents intruding on their family life, but that may be be-

When Adoptions Go Wrong
© 2006 by The Haworth Press, Inc. All rights reserved.
doi:10.1300/5780_06

cause some of the "openness" was limited by the seventh year to an annual holiday greeting and photo rather than frequent visits. Some of the responses seem contradictory, but Siegel was able to explain most of these instances.

A wide range of perspectives exists as to the nature of an open adoption. At minimum, perhaps there may be an exchange of social and demographic information before the adoption or after, but without any identities being revealed. A "semi-open" adoption may involve only the adults, in that they "choose one another and make an arrangement for future contact among themselves" (Rosenberg, 1998, p. 84). In a fully open adoption, all of the adults have to recognize and agree that the adoptive parents are now the child's parents who are primarily responsible for nurturing the child and who make the decisions affecting the child.

The Arizona Children's Association and the Independent Adoption Center in Pleasant Hill, California, both have an open-adoption-only policy for infant adoptions (Hwang, 2004). The birth mother chooses her child's adoptive parents, but the amount of postnatal contact varies from that selection to periodic visits. Although eighteen states have made open adoptions legally enforceable, most state laws also make it almost impossible for the mothers to reclaim their children.

In cases in which the child is a few years old when removed from the biological family, or when the biological and adoptive parents are related in some way (aunts, uncles, grandparents), "open adoption," or continued visitation and other contacts are understandable and even desirable, unless abuse or mental illness has been a factor in the child's removal from the biological parents. However, when the child is adopted as a newborn or very young infant, he or she knows only the adoptive parents and visitation from the biological parents may be confusing and intrusive, depending on when it begins, who is included, and what interaction is involved. In either case, the attorneys, caseworkers, and/or counselors involved need to make the extent of any such arrangement clear to all parties, and to support the best interests of the child (Berry, 1993).

A variation of the "open adoption" format occurs in cases of surrogate mothers who refuse to surrender their parental rights, with the result that the biological father and his wife, who is then limited to being a foster mother, have to share the child with the biological mother.

A major case in point was the "Baby M" case of the mid-1980s (Schwartz, 1986, 1988). In these situations, both the biological mother's family and the biological father's family have to deal with a child who is part of their lives on a court-ordered, part-time basis, and the child is subject to interaction with two, possibly very different, families. In the worst possible outcome for children in this situation, their development "may be subject to conflicting forces in the life space that result in warped emotional development, reduced intellectual functioning, and possible acting-out behavior" (Schwartz, 1993a, p. 271).

"Open adoption" obviously has its proponents, most notably Betty Jean Lifton (1988, 1994), and opponents, as well as those who view that option on a case-by-case basis. Open adoption *can* provide significant health information over the years, and may (or may not) help a child to understand why he or she had been placed for adoption in the first place. Melina and Roszia (1993) have written a very useful guide for those considering open adoption, whether they are the birth parents or the prospective adoptive parents. Another good source is the Web site of the National Adoption Information Clearinghouse (NAIC, 2003a), which has a ten-page "bulletin for professionals" that provides a great deal of information in support of and against open adoptions. The one thing that was not discussed, or even mentioned, in any of these sources was multiple open adoptions within one family. For an illustration of interactions of multiple open adoptions, see Figure 6.1.

Although some open adoptions work well, and there may well be constructive aspects to them, the interaction of more than one set of biological parents (because of more than one adoption in a family) with the children and adoptive parents can lead to disruption of family harmony, if not the adoption itself. The additional parent figures, even if interacting directly only with their own biological child, do have an indirect influence on the other children in the family *and* on the adoptive parents (Schwartz, 2000a). What might be the effects on all in the adoptive family of this input if each of the biological parents has different values, different personalities, and different goals for the children?

Indeed, what might be the effect on all members of the adopted family if the arrangement is an open adoption for some of the children and a closed/traditional one for others? This could quite easily cause friction among the children that might disrupt self-images, self-esteem,

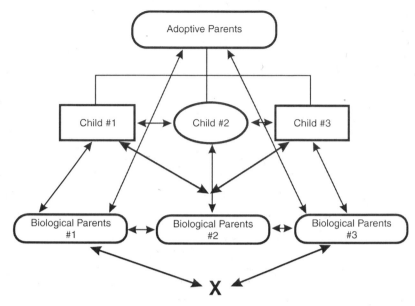

FIGURE 6.1. Interactions of open adoption.

and intrafamily relationships even if the adoptions themselves were not disrupted.

What might be the effect on the adopted family unit and the child(ren) if the caretaking adults and the biological adults disagree on facets of child rearing? For this reason, many would-be adoptive parents have turned to international adoption where such potential complications are less likely to occur (Schwartz & Kaslow, 2003).

In recent years, as will be seen in the following brief discussion of media events, there has been considerable pressure by some agencies and individuals to have an "open" adoption. Katz (2004) provides an interesting discussion of the inconclusive court rulings on that subject in her survey of New York family law. As Katz points out, confirmation of adoption usually terminates any contact with the child's biological relatives, and there is no statutory law dictating otherwise. Indeed, "Consent to adoption which contains a condition of continued visitation has been held not to constitute a valid consent" (Katz, 2004, p. 1133). However, in the case of Gregory B., the boy apparently had a very close relationship with his biological relatives and wanted to maintain contact. The legislature, after consideration of the facts in the case, created an exception to the statute for the boy (p. 1145).

As noted earlier, open adoption may have a negative impact on the adoptive family, especially if there is more than one adopted child, each from different biological parents. On the other hand, given two conditions—(1) no abuse by the biological family, and (2) child of school age or thereabouts at the time of adoption—it might be appropriate for the child to maintain some degree of contact with the biological family as long as it did not generate conflict with the adoptive family. Perhaps the cause for adoption involved the death of the child's parents and the inability of aged or ill grandparents to care for the child. In allowing the child to be adopted, the grandparents were looking out for the child's best interests. Should this mean that they can never see their grandchild again? There should be enough latitude in a statute to enable judges to consider what might be viewed as "exceptions to the rule" with thoughtful recognition of special or unique circumstances. Appell (2003) reports that about eighteen states have enacted some statute regarding adoption with contact, often dependent on the two factors previously mentioned.

A summary of nine articles on open adoption provides a variety of positions regarding this option (Haugaard, West, & Moed, 2000). Although in each case the number of subjects in the study is provided, there is no indication of whether they are from families with one open adoption or multiple open adoptions. As suggested, this difference could certainly affect the success of the adoption.

Media Examples

During the first weekend in May 2004, three examples of open adoption and consequent actual or potential problems were reported in the media. Barbara Walters, on a segment of her *20/20* program called "Be My Baby" (aired on April 30 on the ABC network), highlighted a sixteen-year-old's search for adoptive parents for the baby boy she was carrying—adoptive parents who would allow her to be very much a part of the child's life. Five sets of potential parents were interviewed by the girl *on television,* with her choice being determined by which set would allow her the most access to the child.[1] The potential for disruption should she become too embroiled in the youngster's life as he grows was not even mentioned, but was certainly apparent to psychologists and nonpsychologists alike. That a sixteen-year-old was being allowed to make this decision was not even questioned. Nor was the fact that she was apparently making her decision based on only the one issue, really a kind of emotional greed. There was no hint that she had had any guidance from social workers or other counselors about what else might be important for her baby.

When she gave her baby to the couple she chose, again televised, two or three dozen of her relatives were in the background, and the couple assured her and them that they would all be welcome to visit at any time. How realistic an environment can this be for the child? Or the adoptive parents? It is very easy for someone to aver that the little boy will grow up feeling abundantly loved by his two families, but will he be able to develop a healthy sense of identity and firm attachments to anyone? If he ever should see a tape of the program, how will he feel?

Related to this choice for open adoption was a review of a book titled *Girls in Trouble* by Caroline Leavitt (2004, St. Martin's Press), which also focused on a sixteen-year-old who was pregnant (Trethan, 2004). The girl, who had insisted on an open adoption, became so embroiled with the couple who adopted her baby that her relationship with her own parents became strained. Furthermore, the adoptive parents began to find the teenager very intrusive in their lives, far more involved than they could have envisioned. This certainly demonstrates the extreme situation that can result.

Another example was a television movie made in 1993 (but shown on the *Lifetime* network on May 2, 2004), titled *Moment of Truth: A Child Too Many.* This involved a surrogacy contract that was breached when the would-be parents would only accept one of the twins, a girl, born to the surrogate mother. The other twin, a boy, was to be placed elsewhere, allegedly because the adoptive mother was not strong enough to handle two children (in addition to the biological son she already had). The surrogate mother and her husband fought this separation of the twins and eventually were able to adopt both of them. The disturbance of several lives in the process had a number of similarities to those that occur in disrupted adoptions.

Early in January 2005, the Fox network telecast a program called *Who's My Daddy?* that evoked vehement, though ineffective, protests from adoption organizations as well as individuals. This program depicted a thirty-five-year-old woman who would receive $100,000 if she was able to choose the man who was her biological father from a group of five men. If she erred in her choice, the money would go to the man she chose. One has to wonder about the reasons why any of those involved would choose to participate in such a program, apart, perhaps from the money offered. Certainly, if the woman wanted to locate her father, there were and are other avenues she could follow. As for the biological father, if he had chosen all those years earlier not to be identified, why would he now be willing to do so on live television?

PROFESSIONAL PREVENTION AND INTERVENTION

Basic Knowledge

Nonpsychologists need to recognize that there are many theories regarding how or why children develop as they do. Some emphasize biological ties and others focus on interpersonal interaction and environmental factors. Each theory considers its approach to be the "true" one. The multiple approaches, each of which may lead to a different conclusion, may only serve to confuse the decision maker and perhaps even some of the witnesses in a contested adoption case (Rodham, 1979). It is critical that attorneys working in this field, as well as judges ruling in these cases, know the basic facts of child development, a plea made more than two decades ago (Schwartz, 1983) and equally true today.

Professionals working with a pregnant girl or woman, whether medically or in a social service agency, need to be well-informed about different types of adoption and be able to share that information in an unbiased way with the mother. That is, she needs to know both positive and negative aspects of surrendering her child for adoption, and work with the professionals, perhaps even with a therapist, to determine which format is best for her as well as for the baby she is carrying, at the present time and in the long term. Obviously, the woman must be honest with the professionals helping her with respect to, e.g., whether she is HIV positive, or whether she drank alcohol excessively while pregnant, and/or has other conditions that might place her child at risk.

Professionals working with families *after* adoption have to exercise caution, too.

> Birth parents, adoptive parents, and adoptees share common themes of loss and anger, attachment and separation, and identities that involve paradoxical qualities. . . . Therapists . . . need to understand both the individual client and the interactive aspects of clinical issues in the adoptive family circle. (Rosenberg, 1992, p. 146)

In essence, this means that therapists and others working with individuals or families in the adoptive triangle must be aware of the nature of the adoption, and should neither ignore it, nor overemphasize it. They should look at the problem for which help is being sought and who presents the problem, using appropriate means of assessment to determine its source and means of treatment. They should also look at the state of the parents' marriage and the ability of the couple to work cooperatively to reduce or eliminate the problem. If disruption of the adoption is being contemplated, the therapist must consider that relationship as well as the state of the whole family (Reitz & Watson, 1992).

All professionals involved—mental health, social services, or legal—must be aware of the differences between protracted foster care and legal adoption, between open adoption (and its many variations) and closed adoption, and of the differing developmental levels and perceptions of infants, primary schoolchildren, and adolescents. They must also recognize and support family bonds that exist even when the family is under stress, rather than rushing to remove an adoptee from the adoptive parents, unless there is ongoing abuse.

Legal Changes

It would be helpful, but is unlikely to occur very soon, to have consistent laws throughout a state, and across the country, dealing with when and how a biological mother may surrender her child for adoption, under what circumstances, and within what time limits she can change her mind. Laws were passed in many states requiring biological mothers to notify the child's father or potential father through advertising in a newspaper or by some other method (Barton, 2003; McKenna, 2004; Parness, 2003). One such law, in Florida, required the woman to publish her name, age, description, and description of any men who might have been the child's father, once a week for a month. The law was subsequently declared invalid as a violation of privacy rights (Barton, 2003; McKenna, 2004). It was replaced in Florida by provision for a putative fathers' registry. Under Florida's law, if a man did not register, he waived his right to be notified of court proceedings involving a possible adoption and his consent to the adoption was not required (McKenna, 2004). This placed the burden on the fathers (Binstock, 2004).

Not all states have such registries, and in those that do, they are ineffective on an interstate basis.

> Variations amongst the states as to the breadth of the rights of unwed fathers exist only because the United States Supreme Court has shown a staunch unwillingness to rule decisively on this issue. While the nation's high court is responsible for creating the basic framework of biological father rights, it has avoided elaboration. (Resnik, 1996, p. 380)

The situation has changed very little since Resnik wrote that criticism. In fact, as Beck, a professor of clinical law and an adoption attorney, has written:

> Upholding the constitutional rights of unmarried fathers to their children does not assure that these men will assume parental responsibilities, however. Protecting paternal rights of unmarried fathers without requiring corresponding responsibilities fails to ensure permanent and stable parents for children because unmarried fathers who have no legally defined role in their children's lives have no legal requirements for custody or support. (2002, p. 1033)

Assuming that the alleged father becomes aware of his child, there needs to be a time limitation with respect to when he can assert his status and/or file for termination of *his* rights with respect to a child. On the other hand, for some unwed fathers, registries may not be the appropriate answer, or may be inadequate to the task of informing him properly (Parness, 2003).

All courts need to be cognizant of children's best interests. The Family Law Section of the American Bar Association adopted a resolution in 1991 encouraging the appointment of a guardian-ad-litem in all disputed custody cases if this is necessary to protect those interests (Elrod, 1996, ch. 12, p. 3, n. 10). If adopted children, of whatever tender age, are to be regarded as persons rather than possessions, they should be so represented by an advocate in any hearings. A detailed proposal for such representation is offered in the next chapter.

The Uniform Adoption Act (UAA), adopted in 1994 by The National Conference of Commissioners on State Laws, was an attempt to clarify the rights of all parties. It also focused on recognition that adoptive families are the legal equivalent of biological families, and that, in the event of controversy, the child is the party with the most at stake. Parts or all of the Uniform Adoption Act have been adopted in many states, but not all (1995). The act attempted to reduce or remove many of the causes for protracted litigation with its negative effects on all parties, but especially the children. Among the provisions of the UAA are the following:

1. Anyone may adopt. (This includes homosexuals, cohabiting couples, single persons, and others presently prevented from so doing in some jurisdictions.)
2. Birth parents may select adoptive parents. (This permits a better exchange of information, and possibly an "open" adoption, whether by independent or agency placement.)
3. Adoptive parents must receive a positive pre-placement evaluation.
4. Clarified consent requirements for both biological and adoptive parents, and limitations on revocation of consent (192 hours), as well as provisions for the unmarried father to be informed.
5. Appointment of an attorney as advocate for the child in custody litigation.
6. Implicit, sometimes expressed, focus on the "best interests of the child."
7. Encourages counseling for birth parents. (Wambaugh, 1999, pp. 816-831)

According to Tenenbaum (1996), critics of the UAA contend that the act "emphasizes the 'rights of adults' instead of the 'best interests of children.' This is simply not true" (p. 336). He also pointed out that the act "looks to a child's best interests by adding a provision that allows a minor child's foster, de facto, or psychological parents standing to adopt the child, subject to the particular child's needs" (p. 336).

Lowe (1996) examines the UAA in relation to the parental rights doctrine which, if stiffly or rigidly applied, "results in the destruction of a 'true and loving' family in the name of protecting a biological family that did not even exist at the time the child's ties to her nonbiological parents were forged" (p. 381). Lowe further considers that the parental rights doctrine

> has two fundamental flaws. On the one hand, it ignores the reality of a family as it is actually experienced by children whose primary attachment is to a non-biological parent. . . . At the same time, the parental rights doctrine devalues caregiving and that which flows from it . . . (pp. 384-385)

The Uniform Adoption Act was passed and many of the comments about it were made during the turmoil of the Baby Jessica and Baby Richard cases. Standing back from the media hyperbole a decade later, and even from the court rulings of that period, it becomes more and more apparent that each case must be decided on its unique circumstances.

SUMMARY

Although the Supreme Court has recognized fundamental rights of parenthood, it "has also recognized that parental rights are not absolute. In extreme cases in which parental rights conflict with the best interests of the child, parental rights may even be terminated" (Portwood & Repucci, 1994, pp. 11-12). At the same time, recognition of the role of psychological parents, and the strength of the resulting parent-child relationship, is and should be a critical factor considered in determining whose rights should prevail in contested adoption custody cases. Families are created by caring interaction and relationships, not solely or even primarily by biology. Professionals should have as much concern and respect for the rights of the child and his or her caretakers as for the rights of those who created that baby. However, each case, each family, must be evaluated in its own right and with consideration of its unique history and circumstances.

Chapter 7

Where Do We Go From Here?

Adoption disruption *is* a negative life event for almost all the people directly involved. The ways in which they respond during the turmoil and how they let it affect their lives in the long term obviously depend on their personalities, their past experiences, and indeed even events that occur later in their lives. We know relatively little about the long-term effects on the children, for they are rarely heard of again unless there is some newsworthy event in their lives. In the major cases presented here, the children are still too young to be able to seek out their would-be adoptive parents on their own, if they are even aware of their existence. Clearly, there is a great deal that we do not know about their lives. What we can do, however, is try to reduce the incidence of such disruptions.

PREVENTIVE MEASURES

Transfer of Custody

In the Baby Richard and Baby Jessica cases, judges were so concerned about restoring these children to their biological parents that they ignored the "child's best interests." It would have been better for the children, possibly more difficult for all the parents involved, to have had some supervised visitation sessions prior to the transfer so that the children would at least have met the "new" parents, rather than being handed over like a package—a thing. A move in that direction was seen in the Evan Scott case, although there was no indication that the visit with Evan's biological mother was a supervised one.

Scarnecchia, who represented the DeBoers in the Baby Jessica case, deplored the absence of the child's right to due process "when

When Adoptions Go Wrong
© 2006 by The Haworth Press, Inc. All rights reserved.
doi:10.1300/5780_07

state action, in the form of a transfer of custody, is likely to cause substantial harm to the child" (1995, p. 46). The harm, as Scarnecchia phrased it, is "transfer trauma" due to the abrupt separation from those she knows to a new home with strangers. She argues, "children have a constitutionally protected right to liberty in the form of security from state-imposed harm, including substantial harm to their psychological and emotional welfare" (Scarnecchia, 1995, p. 46).

In addition to facilitating the transfer of the child, it might be helpful to the child, and even the nonbiological caretakers, if some continuing contact is maintained after the transfer and as the child matures. Even if contact occurs only a couple of times a year, perhaps interspersed with notes and photos, the child would not feel abandoned by the psychological parents and they could at least feel a bit less bereft.

The Putative Father Problem

As mentioned earlier, several states have enacted statutes providing for putative father registries. They vary from one state to another and may not be effective in cases involving interstate moves. Beck (2002) asserted that Congress should enact a national putative father database that would both enable registered unmarried fathers to be notified of pending adoption proceedings and contribute to more secure adoption placements. A national database, in an area normally left to the states, would safeguard fathers' rights in the event that the mother has moved from one state to another. Such a database would not only include information about the father, but also "name and last known address of the mother, location of possible conception, month(s) and/or year(s) of possible conception, birth date of child or expected delivery date, name and gender and birth date of the child if known" (Beck, 2002, p. 1076). A "Chart of State Statutes Describing Paternity Registries" appended to Beck's article demonstrates the wide variability among the states in requirements for time limits and consequences for failure to file (pp. 1079-1080). (One wonders how many men will be willing to register their sexual activity, even if they are supposed to, under the law.) However, "The act of registering provides the most feasible and effective way for the unknown biological father to meet the Supreme Court's requirement of demonstrating a full commitment to the responsibilities of parenthood" (Barton, 2003, p. 145).

Follow-Up to the Baby Jessica Case

The Baby Jessica case, the Baby Richard case, and the Baby Emily case, all discussed in earlier chapters, provoked many calls for changes in adoption laws (Rosenman, 1995), some of which have occurred. Particular attention, in the wake of these cases and even earlier, was paid to the role and rights of unwed fathers with respect to the adoption of newborns (Resnik, 1996; Schwartz, 1986), but did not always result in revisions of existing statutes. Indeed, some of the revisions that did occur were designed hastily and in response to a barrage of media attention. Yet another Fourteenth Amendment issue to be resolved is whether children are fully protected under the equal protection clause and have full citizenship rights in matters that affect their lives in the most profound way.

A contrary position was taken in a case by the New York State Court of Appeals. An unmarried father sought to upset the adoption of a son of whose existence he was unaware for the child's first eighteen months of life (Hevesi, 1992). His then ex-fiancée had not told him she was pregnant. The court ruled "that the child's welfare, the rights of the adoptive parents, the attachments developed in that family and the state's interest in maintaining the integrity of adoptions must take precedence" (Hevesi, 1992, p. B6). The court, although recognizing that the biological father had acted promptly when he became aware of his paternity status, acted in accord with the baby's best interests. In this case, obviously, the child was seen as a person, not a possession, and with appropriate recognition of the difference in perception of time by children and adults.

The New York Court of Appeals had ruled in an earlier case that a statutory requirement that "a putative father live with the mother for a portion, if not all, of the six months prior to adoption to earn the right to veto that adoption" was invalid (Zinman, 1992, p. 972). This ruling left the courts somewhat in a muddle. Either they granted custody to a deserving father, risking emotional harm to his child, or approved the adoption and deprived the putative father of his rights (Zinman, 1992). Clearly, as would be seen repeatedly in many courts, there is no easy answer to such a problem.

Upgraded Social and Legal Agency Services

Two papers, in particular, have been focused on the placement of older children into permanent homes, a challenge for social service agencies as well as the child and the receiving family. One emphasizes the need for a better psychological evaluation, using full test batteries rather than academically oriented batteries alone, of the older child or adolescent, to be carried out by an individual properly trained in this area (Kirby & Hardesty, 1998). The other stresses the need to evaluate the receiving family so that there will be a better fit between the older child and the family (Ward, 1997).

With an older child, clearly there is a history that should be available to the psychologist doing an evaluation. This should include any birth problems, how long the child was with the biological parent(s) and the nature of the parent-child relationhip, any special needs, and the child's experience through any foster care placements and court hearings. Why was the child placed in foster care? For how long? If the child was moved, why? A psychologist needs to have answers to these questions in order to make a solid recommendation for future adoption. Kirby and Hardesty (1998) also stress the need to interview the child and, if the child's version of experiences differs from the archival record, to follow up after the interview to obtain a clarification of the discrepancies. Certainly the child's perception of families and experiences will affect motivation, expectations of the next family, ability to attach to the new family, and reduced probability of adoption disruption.

Ward (1997) examines the other end of the situation. She describes a variety of family types or paradigms, beginning with "closed families" which are fairly traditional, and which "meet members' needs by providing stability, structure, and a sense of belonging" (Ward, 1997, p. 259). These families may be appropriate for incoming sibling groups, or some emotionally disturbed children. By contrast, what she calls "random families" are more permissive and encourage individual efforts to achieve or to solve problems. These families would be good for an incoming child who is well-motivated, but less so for a child with serious physical or other problems. Then there are "open" families that emphasize communication and family-based activities; "synchronous" families that value harmony in the family, albeit attaining it through nonverbal communication; and "intermediate and misaligned families," in which husband and wife have different styles that may pose difficulties for the children, biological or adopted (Ward, 1997). Each has strengths that will aid some older adoptees, but other facets of their style will not provide as good a match. The social agency worker, or the intermediary, must ascertain both the youth's needs and the family's paradigm to reduce the possibility of an adoption disruption. This is a different kind of matchmaking, and it takes training and sensitivity to do it effectively. It also calls for continuing support from the social service agency.

Barth and Miller (2000) write

> The extent and nature of the need for post-adoption services will depend in large part on two factors: (a) whether adopted children have unusual needs by virtue of the amount or type of problems they have and (b) whether these needs can be met by existing approaches to service delivery. (p. 348)

Barth and Miller reviewed four postadoption studies and found that family therapy/counseling services were helpful in reducing adoption disruptions, even when the children were older, had been victims of physical or sexual abuse, or had one or more special needs. In some cases, simply providing information helped; in others, financial aid to support needed medical care was the key to maintaining the adoption. Even more helpful would be multifaceted programs that involve community aspects and a lighter (e.g., ten cases) and more actively involved caseload for the agency workers.

Yet another suggestion is to revive congregate or institutional care (Ladner, 2000).

> There are more children than ever in foster care, too few social workers and potential adoptive parents, a declining number of potential foster families, and fewer children being returned to their biological families. The question is what to do with children who are unlikely either to be reunited with their parents or adopted. (p. 6)

The type of institutional care Ladner proposes would provide education as well as housing, and would be staffed by highly trained professionals. It might be comprised of a number of mini "villages" with professionals serving as parent figures or, as Ladner mentions, re-semble Girard College in Philadelphia, a boarding school founded in the nineteenth century, which cares for more than 600 children in grades one through twelve.

Independent adoption is perceived in different ways at different times and by different people. Certainly, it has been seen by would-be adoptive parents as an alternative to working with adoption agencies with their restrictions on who may adopt and long waiting lists. The intermediary or facilitator in independent adoptions is often an attor-ney. The attorneys, however, need to avoid conflicts of interest. They cannot represent both the would-be parents and the mother-to-be, or, if representing the prospective parents, give her advice about the con-sequences of her consent to having her baby adopted (Amlung, 1990). On the other hand, if they are representing the mother-to-be, they need to advise her on the statutes in her state regarding whether she can change her mind once she signs a form terminating her paren-tal rights, and if so, what time limits exist for her doing so. These vary from one state to another, and sometimes within states. As well-meaning as attorneys may be, they, like psychologists, cannot fill two functions in the same case.[1]

Today there is an abundance of information about helpful agen-cies, policies, and laws available on Web sites. Two sites that may be especially helpful to professionals are www.nationalcasa.org and www.masskids.org. The first site leads to information on court-appointed special advocates (CASA); the second site has links to adoption, advocacy, foster care, legal, and other resources across the country (e.g., Illinois, Maryland, Michigan, New York, Utah), al-though the heading on several of its pages is "Massachusetts Citizens for Children." The CASA home page states its purpose very clearly: one-half of the page shows a photo of a girl, probably age eleven or twelve, with her eyes looking straight into the viewer's eyes; the other half reads: "Sara is in foster care. She's been moved 11 times in 2 years. She would rather live on the street." Then, a piece of chalk overwrites the text, with an arrow pointing to the "11 times," and reads "CASA volunteer steps in here." The frequent moves, almost every other month over a two-year period, reflects what Bowman's (1995) inter-viewees told her.

Limits on Time to Make Decisions

> State legislatures have seemingly been unable to draft statutes
> with the requisite clarity for courts to be able to readily resolve
> these conflicts in a manner expeditious enough to avoid wreak-
> ing havoc upon the lives of the prospective adoptive parents, the
> natural fathers, and the children they fight over. . . . And once
> disagreements over statutory interpretation arise, the judicial
> system has proved itself to be too cumbersome to resolve these
> disputes in a timely manner. (Resnik, 1996, pp. 378-379)

These criticisms were written after the Baby Jessica, Baby Richard, Baby Emily, and other cases had dragged on and on and on.
Resnik (1996) further asserted that these cases demonstrated an "in-
escapable paradox," in that adoption is supposed to work for the best
interests of the child, while some of the courts, when judging the
rights of unmarried fathers who are contesting the adoption, refuse to
consider those best interests. Indeed, as we have seen in several of the
cases discussed, many months, and sometimes a year or more, may
pass before a court hands down its decision. Is this fair to anyone?

In 2002, a case in Michigan was in the appeals court for eight
months and then in the state's supreme court for more than a year
(Anonymous, 2004b). As the (unknown) author of the newspaper article wrote: "When a child's future is at stake, especially in the most
formative years, time must be of the essence in settling permanency
issues" (Anonymous, 2004b). The author urged that appeals of TPR
cases take no more than eleven months total—eight in the court of appeals and three in the supreme court.[2]

One of the facts that needs to be recognized by all parties is that a
young child's sense of time differs considerably from that of adults.
One example is the Baby Richard case. In a particularly harsh criticism of the court in that case, Heldman (2003) cited the finding of the
Illinois Supreme Court that its state laws regarding adoption were not
complex. Heldman asked, "why did it take more than three years to
decide such a simple application of law while a child continued to be
raised by two 'parents' he would never see again?" (p. 1003). Apparently, the justice who handed down the opinion blamed the delay in
resolving the case "on the biological mother, the adoptive parents,
and even the attorney for the adoptive parents. However, the court

avoided any acknowledgement of its own failure to provide Richard with a timely resolution" (p. 1003).

If judges will not, or cannot, act on their own to set reasonable time limits for decision making in cases involving the welfare of children, then it behooves every state legislature to enact new rules. Certainly a judge hearing a case has become familiar with the arguments and evidence during the course of the trial. One has to allow the judge time to verify cases cited in the arguments and allegations made about the character or characteristics of the biological parent seeking to prevent the adoption of his or her child. Access to much of that information has been tremendously accelerated by the availability of legal cases on the Internet, as well as speedy electronic transmission of personal records. Today there is very little excuse for a judge to need more than thirty days to reach and announce a decision. If the decision is then appealed, and there should be a similar time limitation for that to occur, then the appellate court should render its decision within thirty days.

Justice Gerald Kogan of the Supreme Court of Florida, in his opinion on the Baby Emily case

> entreated the Family Law Rules Committee of The Florida Bar, and the Florida Legislature, to study methods of expediting contested adoption cases, and noted that "lawsuits of this type cry out for at least four broad reforms: (1) expedited review in the trial court; (2) expedited appeal; (3) swift and certain finality of court decisions; and (4) reasonable mechanisms to minimize psychological harm to the child during the legal process." (Eisen, 1998, pp. 344-345)

The case plan would include a court order setting forth the specifics of "time, manner, and conditions for transfer of custody" (p. 381) which would occur no less than five days after the case was finalized. Unfortunately, what is not specifically included in this proposal is a transition stage preceding final transfer of custody, a stage that might begin on the fifth day following a final decision and continue for at least three to four weeks.

Indeed, cases of this nature should have first priority in the courts, higher than any other case except perhaps those involving a stay of a death sentence or something of that magnitude. Children's entire lives are affected by the decisions being made. As Heldman (2003) has also pointed out, the courts *can* move quickly if the issue is a child's *physical* well-being, as when parents object to a blood transfusion that goes against religious convictions (and freedom of religion). The child's psychological well-being should be no less important. The courts (and legislatures) need to understand that decisions in this realm are totally different than deciding, e.g., whether a corporate officer is 25 percent responsible for the faults of his or her company. The focus here is on children's lives and their future well-being. As a society, there is a clear responsibility to reduce the disadvantages to children, and to demonstrate that we value them.

A True Family Court

Who represents the children?

In many, perhaps most, jurisdictions in the United States, different courts hear cases involving different aspects of family problems. Divorce suits are often heard in one court and adoption disputes in another. In addition, too often, any children involved are not represented by a child advocate. Mason (1994), among others, recommends that *all* family matters be heard in one true family court, *with* representation for the children involved, continuing counseling available for the children and families, and periodic review of the custody arrangements to be sure that they are working in a positive way.

In 2003, the American Bar Association House of Delegates approved a revision of its Family Law section's standards on representing children. Although the focus was mainly on children in cases where the parents were divorcing and in dispute about custody, obviously the representation of children in adoption cases is also affected. The new standards abolish the role of guardian-ad-litem, and instead create two possible roles for lawyers involved in custody cases:

> (1) a "Child's Attorney," with all the ethical duties of an attorney-client relationship, including confidentiality and loyalty to the client's decisions and objectives, or (2) a "Best Interests Attorney," who independently investigates and advocates the child's best interests, as a lawyer. A lawyer can do either of these, but not both in the same case. (Crouch, 2003, p. 6)

The "Child's Attorney" is an advisor as well as an advocate; the "Best Interests Attorney," among other things, conveys the child's desires to the court if the child so desires. Both types of lawyers will take courses in child custody and visitation law as well as a number of other related topics. The ABA "Standards of Practice" (2003) very clearly states that lawyers in these roles must have training in "children's development, needs and abilities at different ages, communicating with children, preparing and presenting a child's viewpoints, including child testimony and alternatives to direct testimony," and "multidisciplinary input required in child-related cases, including information on local experts who can provide evaluation, consultation and testimony" (pp. 22-23). These requirements are a commendable step forward for the Family Law section, and should result in much improved representation for children caught in the middle of family disputes, whether divorce or adoption.

A "Unified" Family Court

In recent years there have been efforts to have the same judge hear all cases involving a family, rather than one hearing one problem and another hearing a different issue, so that judgments are rendered on the basis of full information (Festinger & Pratt, 2002). This seems to make good sense, in that it would reduce the likelihood of a party being able to hide relevant information involving anyone in the case at hand. One such model is the "unified family court" which

> provides for comprehensive subject matter jurisdiction over all types of family law cases—from divorce to child protection to adoption—and implements a "one family, one judge" docket structure that consolidates a family's multiple legal and social problems" with an eye to therapeutic as well as legal resolution. (Developments in the Law, 2003, p. 2099; see also Bozzomo & Scolieri, 2004; Wu, 2002)

LAWS ACROSS THE LAND

Two decades ago, Lowery (1984) pointed out the differences in the perspectives that mental health professionals bring to custody cases and those of the judiciary. Although she was considering primarily custody conflicts in divorce, her point of view may be equally applicable to contested adoption cases. Lowery asserted that the former ask "Which parent is a better match for having primary responsibility for raising the child?," while the latter are more likely to ask "Which parent is a better adult?" (p. 379). This difference contributed in some measure to the high-profile disruptions that have been discussed in this book. A decade later, because of these cases and others, serious attempts have been made to reduce the difference.

In the aftermath of the Baby Jessica and Baby Richard cases, for example, a fair amount of scrambling occurred among people in several related professions to try to find ways to prevent such grievous cases from recurring. Scarnecchia, who had represented the DeBoers and who was a clinical law professor, made a number of recommendations for reforming state laws to provide certain guarantees regarding adoptions:

1. Children's cases should be heard and decided quickly.
2. If the adults in a child's life cannot determine his or her custody satisfactorily, "then the court must be permitted to consider how the proposed custody arrangement directly affects the child" (Scarnecchia, 1994, p. 11).
3. The law "must acknowledge the very real parent-child relationships that can exist between children and nonbiological parents" and give the latter the "right to sue for custody" (Scarnecchia, 1994, p. 11).

Scarnecchia also recommended limitations on the rights of nonbiological parents to sue for custody, especially when the child was in an intact biological home, but she added that "there should never be a rule that biological parents can automatically repossess their children *like property,* without any reference to how the change of custody will affect the live little person involved" (1994, p. 12, italics added).

A family court judge (Kreeger, 2003) and a family law practitioner (Kirkland, 2003), in response to a special journal issue on family psychology and family law, both commented that there have been many changes in society and medicine in recent years of which family court personnel are apparently unaware, and to which the law has not been adapted. This makes it less likely that judges and lawyers will realize the probable negative impact on children (and families) of some of their decisions. "Traditional family law principles are inadequate to address these issues," asserted Kreeger (2003, p. 262), and he called on policymakers to correct the situation.

Mediation

Mediation in divorce cases is mandatory in some states, and is a growing alternative to prolonged litigation (Mason, 1994). It is an approach that might be used in adoption disputes as well to reduce the level of conflict affecting all the parties, most critically, of course, the children. Not only is the level of conflict reduced, but the financial costs to all parties would also be substantially reduced, despite most parents' ardent claim that they would spend "everything I have" to keep their child.

Landsman, Thompson, and Barber (2003) have written a detailed account of a mediation program developed in Iowa to expedite the settlement of foster care arrangements, adoptions, and termination of parental rights with more cooperation and agreement among parties than bitterness. The Iowa Mediation for Permanency Project has "permanency" as a key goal, recognizes the importance of attachments, allows for some flexibility in timing, uses a nonadversarial approach, and promotes collaboration among the parties. It is, perhaps, most useful when the child of concern is involved with a social service agency, in foster care, or more permanent placement. Like another mediation project developed earlier in Oregon, it reduces litigation while allowing all parties to be heard. The Iowa project, however, encourages mediation at any point in the placement process rather than only in connection with termination of parental rights.

The mediators were selected from a number of related fields (social work, law, mental health) and culturally diverse backgrounds. They had to have at least three years' experience working with children and their families in the child welfare system, and had to complete a mediation training course geared to child welfare issues. They had to "have knowledge of the juvenile court system, the child welfare system, and an understanding of the complexity of the dynamics the families experienced" (Landsman, Thompson, & Babrer, 2003, p. 233). They also had to be neutral in the decision making, and were allowed neither to testify for or against any of the parties in court. Their job was to help negotiate a workable and mutually acceptable agreement among the parties. They also were able to educate case-workers and communities about the mediation approach to achieve permanency for the children involved.

Mediation may actually be more appropriate to some adoption cases than others, perhaps more with an older child who would actually have strong ties with and memories of his or her biological family. The mediator might be able to assist the parties to reach an agreement on how much contact there should be between the two families. Depending on the age of the child involved, he or she might also contribute to the negotiations, and certainly ought to heard by the mediator.

RECOGNITION OF PSYCHOLOGICAL VERSUS BIOLOGICAL PARENTING

Among biological children, there may well be situations in which they feel that a nonparent, whether an extended family member or a nonmember, is "like a mother to me." She, for example, is the one, rather than the biological mother, to whom the child or adolescent goes with questions and problems, and is the one who provides answers and comfort. The same may be true with a father figure who provides more guidance or help of one kind or another than the youth's actual father. This is the underlying relationship of psychological parenting. The child or adolescent in this situation tries to model his or her behavior on that of the psychological parent's example, and to gain that adult's approval and respect.

If this is true for biological children, it is more true for adopted children who have been raised and nurtured by their adoptive parents. Even if they search adoption records as young adults and eventually meet their biological parents, or if the biological parent tracks them down, there is little basis for the parent-child attachment that develops through shared life experiences. Nineteen youths, age eight to sixteen years, commented on their adoption and prior backgrounds and not one indicated a preference for the biological parents (Krementz, 1993). Some were in mixed-race adoptive families; a couple of them had biological siblings from whom they had been separated, although one had been adopted with her twin brother; only two expressed feelings of rejection or low self-image; all but one voiced strong positive feelings toward their adoptive parents.

Wambaugh (1999) suggests that "biological attachment" does not exist when a child is placed as an infant and never knew his or her biological progenitors.

> If courts refuse to acknowledge this, they can more easily deny children standing in the proceedings that directly affect their lives. . . . The presumption that biology is best, does not place enough emphasis on the care-giving performed by the child's "psychological parents." (Wambaugh, 1999, p. 808)

Psychologists testifying in a case involving a three-and-a-half-year-old girl, for example, testified that she would be traumatized if removed from her foster mother and would suffer irreparable and permanent emotional and developmental damage (Dyer, 1999).

It may be interesting, even pleasurable, for adoptees to meet members of their extended biological family, but they will not have childhood memories to share or common experiences on which to base a continuing relationship. If they are fortunate enough to find a sibling, a cousin, or other relative with whom they share interests or talents, and begin a friendship, this is still not based on biology. As an example, one woman, then in her mid-thirties, contacted the social welfare agency by which she had been placed as an infant, and, with the consent of her biological mother was reunited with her. The initial meeting took place at the agency's offices, with two of the woman's half-siblings, who had remained living with the mother, waiting downstairs "just in case anything went wrong." Mother and daughter hit it off well, and the younger woman then met all four of her half-siblings. She became quite friendly with one of them, based on common interests. The mother died two years later, and the daughter still feels pleased that they had been in contact during that period (Author's case files).

SUMMARY

Varying laws and practices have contributed to stress and distress for many children caught in the web of adoption disruption. In this chapter, a number of potential preventive measures have been suggested that might reduce the number of negative outcomes in these situations. They do not all require changes in statutes, but personnel involved are obligated to enhance their knowledge of development and psychological relationships, broaden their perspectives, and modify some of their practices.

Epilogue

Adoption is, in one sense, a triangular affair, with the adoptive parents, the biological parents, and the children each contributing a facet to the whole. In this book, we have moved from positive contributions that create a family to a study of actions that can destroy a family, and the effects that these have on all members of the triangle. As these behaviors were explored in more detail, it was disturbing to confirm the impotence of the children involved in these cases in almost every situation. It was and is disconcerting to find out how *their* lives and welfare are too frequently disrupted by biological parents who, e.g., tell each other lies about the child's birth to offset their own grievances with each other. The lies then lead to furthering the disruption by caseworkers, legislators, and jurists who deliberately or otherwise misinterpret or misapply laws that were passed to protect the children. As is true in many other areas of life, the adult parties involved in contested adoptions are too quick to litigate rather than seek to mitigate the situation and, as we have already noted, the courts take too long to issue their rulings, so that the children—innocent parties in the controversies—are the ones to suffer.

For many years, I and others have urged that children always have an advocate whose sole role is to represent their position and their needs. If nothing else, it is my fervent hope that politicians and legislators will recognize that, although they can't vote, children have rights, a key one of which is to be represented in any legal matter that involves or affects them. Laws should be passed promptly in every state and territory mandating the appointment of an independent child advocate, whether a "Child's Attorney" or a "Best Interests Attorney," for every child in cases that affect them, and there can be no denying that foster care and adoption are such cases. Then (and one has to hope that it might take only a year or two, not decades), provi-

When Adoptions Go Wrong
© 2006 by The Haworth Press, Inc. All rights reserved.
doi:10.1300/5780_08

sion for mediation might be enacted, jurists might recognize that they ought to issue their rulings in a more timely manner, and everyone might realize that if we give our children better care in their early years, we might be able to reduce the emotional instability and negative behaviors in adolescence and adulthood that too frequently are the result of a disrupted childhood.

Three other factors in studying adoption disruption were not found in any reference in the law review articles, psychology/psychiatry articles or books, and even the nonprofessional literature. One was the consideration, in families that practiced "open adoption," of the potential complications of having more than one adopted child (except for the study by Barth & Brooks, 1997) and more than one "open adoption" in the same family. "Birth parents, adoptive parents, and adoptees share common themes of loss and anger, attachment and separation, and identities that involve paradoxical qualities. . . . Therapists . . . need to understand both the individual client and the interactive aspects of clinical issues in the adoptive family circle" (Rosenberg, 1992, p. 146). Have researchers simply focused only on one child in a family? Or selected for their samples only families with one adopted child? If so, is this realistic? I don't think so.

The second factor was the apparent frequent, almost routine, absence of judicial recognition of the needs of the child being moved from one home to another—whether one foster home to another, or foster/adoptive care back to unknown biological parents—to have a transition period for the child to become acquainted with his or her new caretakers. Rarely has this been part of a court's ruling. Biology does not create an instant attachment, nor does it make the child eradicate the psychological parents from his or her mind instantaneously, although this obviously depends upon the child's age to some degree.

Related to the second factor is the third—the effects of a forced change of name. Perhaps there is not enough awareness of this when a child is moved, or not enough documentation, but it is a critical change for the child and worth studying.

Wrenching a child away from the known to the unknown is traumatic. This would be so even for adults. In the maze of adoption disruption, focus on the *child's* best interests too often is somehow lost. We need to rediscover or to create better ways to minimize the risks to children's lives and mental health. We also need to recognize that one format may not fit all cases. There needs to be informed flexibility, within legal parameters, among the decision makers, so that the needs of the child and his or her multiple parents can be met most effectively and with minimal damage to all parties.

Notes

Chapter 1

1. This continues to be a source of frequent and prolonged litigation more than twenty years later.

2. The extension of various rights enjoyed by married homosexual couples may be extended to same-sex partners in some states, but which rights in which states is a situation very much in flux in the middle of the first decade of the twenty-first century.

3. Transracial placement, while far more common today than even a decade ago, remains a source of controversy in many sectors. Some of the controversy has declined, however, as more Asian children have been adopted, and people in larger communities become more accustomed to seeing multiethnic families.

4. An increasing number of pediatricians are specializing in just such work.

Chapter 2

1. He is apparently a strong supporter of Concerned United Birthparents, an organization founded by a young woman who had been adopted, sought information about her birth parents, and believes that information about them should be readily available to adoptees. He is also Executive Director of the Evan B. Donaldson Adoption Institute.

2. Apparently, this would have been handled differently had it occurred in Michigan rather than Iowa (State Bar of Michigan, 2001).

3. That ruling in itself was highly controversial as the mother was not found abusive, but rather she had prejudiced the twins against their father—her partner who admitted committing adultery against his wife (Sherman & Port, 2004).

4. As of March 6, 2006, no decision regarding (Wecker) Conley was available.

Chapter 3

1. In California alone, between 1983 and 1987, "courts annulled sixty-nine adoptions because adoption agencies fraudulently misrepresented the physical or mental health history of the adopted child" (Bebensee, 1993, p. 398).

2. Who in "the agency" actually made this decision? Was there no individual responsibility?

When Adoptions Go Wrong
© 2006 by The Haworth Press, Inc. All rights reserved.
doi:10.1300/5780_09

3. In addition, one must consider that, although what these authors say has a certain truth, the comments were written at the height of the Baby Richard and Baby Jessica controversies in the early 1990s.

Chapter 4

1. Otto had married Richard's mother during the legal struggle, but left her and Richard in 1996 (Nordgren, 1997).

2. Author's comment: Like so many others who watched the transfer of Baby Richard on April 30, 1995, I can still see it, complete with the mass of media personnel and equipment. The tears of a puzzled, slightly older brother, John, are equally vivid in my memory. What Baby Richard was experiencing, as well as his adoptive family, seemed outrageous. When I became aware of Moriarty's book as I was writing this, I immediately read it in hopes of clarifying those memories.

Karen Moriarty, PhD, is a licensed clinical psychologist who became a pro bono therapist to the Kirchners and Danny for the first year after his return, and has remained their friend and confidante for the past several years. (Her background includes a doctorate in counselor education, followed by a postdoctoral year of study, and a two-day written state examination to achieve licensing status [Moriarty, 2003, p. 66].) She has written an extraordinarily detailed history of the fight over Richard/Danny, much of it apparently based on detailed notes she made in case she was ever called to testify about the boy's adjustment to and treatment by his biological parents. In an effort to clarify some of the points she made, a timetable of events is shown in this chapter.

Even if I were to accept only half of what Moriarty wrote about the Warburtons' behavior over the years as well as that of the Kirchners, the book would still be a strong indictment of the Warburtons, a journalist named Bob Greene, the behavior of some of the attorneys involved, and the almost incomprehensible time lapses in the courts between the filing of an appeal and the decision on it. Moriarty spends a great many pages lambasting Bob Greene, who allegedly wrote some 50,000 words in sixty-six columns both before and after Richard's transfer (Olsen, 1995) (or 100 columns according to another journalist who counted them over a longer period [Steinberg, 2002]), including four columns in which he criticized Moriarty and raised questions about her credentials, costing her most of her private practice as well as investigations by Illinois credentialing authorities and the American Psychological Association. (Olsen and Steinberg's accounts are secondary sources, so there is room for error in either direction.) Most of Greene's columns, however, attacked Otto, the biological father, with the alleged result that he could not obtain employment for two years or more. In that period, he became the primary caretaker of his son, while Daniella worked and earned the family's income.

As I read Moriarty, I began to wonder whether she was possibly overreacting or exaggerating, so I went searching for data that might answer that question. Bruce Boyer, who helped draft Otto's initial appeal to the Illinois Supreme Court, and who also worked pro bono, has since written, "In much of the commentary calling for reform of custody laws, insufficient regard has been paid to the protections of due process that, ultimately, guard against the inevitable risk of governmental interference with families whose gravest offense is their failure to conform" (Boyer & Lubet,

2000, p. 246). In a sense, Otto and Daniella's problems of nonconformity stemmed from a combination of their naiveté and their lack of knowledge of American, especially Illinois, law. When Daniella consented to the termination of her parental rights, she did not know that she could rescind that within a limited number of hours, nor that years later, she would be unable to have that TPR overturned. She sought the reversal in part because she was actually Danny's mother and caring for him in that role, and, second, because both she and Otto were concerned about possible actions if anything happened to him. Indeed, once news of her petition to vacate the consent appeared in the media, the Warburtons' attorneys allegedly filed "a petition with the court on their behalf, arguing that Daniella 'intentionally inflicted severe emotional harm' on them by allowing Danny's adoption and then trying to undo it" (Moriarty, 2003, p. 339). (This was more than two years after the boy was returned to Otto and Daniella.)

With respect to Moriarty's allegations of noncooperation (to say the least) by the Warburtons, Boyer and Lubet cite the hiding of Richard's birth from his father "as a result of both the mother's refusal to cooperate with efforts to notify the father and affirmative misrepresentations to the court by the adoptive parents and their lawyer about the father's status" (2000, p. 258). In the written opinion of the Illinois Supreme Court ruling of January 25, 1995, the justices

> harshly criticized the Warburtons for keeping the child, accusing them of "deceit and subterfuge" in keeping Kirchner from his son. The opinion stated that "On June 6, 1991, (when Kirchner's attorney made a court appearance), the Warburtons had both a legal and a moral duty to surrender Richard to the custody of his father. . . . They have prolonged these painful proceedings to the child's fourth birthday and have denied [Kirchner] any access to his own son." (White, 1997c)

Other than this quotation, the general tone of White's summaries of the case (1997a,b,c) are very pro-Warburton, and, incidentally, negative toward Moriarty (White, 1997b).

There is no doubt that children are frequently the victims of what Lubet describes as "a severe tension in modern juvenile law between those who assert the primacy of 'parental rights' and those who focus on the 'best interests of the child'" (1999, p. 969). This seems most apparent, he continued, "in situations where birth parents are attempting to overturn a completed (or nearly completed) adoption" (Lubet, 1999, p. 969). The statement is particularly apt in the Baby Richard case where one side misrepresented or omitted information, the courts took a great deal of time to render any decisions, and the boy was the innocent victim of both lies and inertia, as well as intensive media coverage. From what was observed, through September 2003, however, he has apparently weathered the storms well, and certainly looks like an athletic, well-fed, and handsome early adolescent in the photos included in the book (Moriarty, 2003).

3. Whether or not one agrees with the decision, he is to be congratulated as one of the few to set up a transition phase that permits the child to become acquainted with her biological parents over time rather than via an abrupt turnover.

4. That four boys, only two of whom were biologically related, all suffered from similar eating disorders seems unlikely, although that was what was claimed by Raymond and Vanessa Jackson, their adoptive parents.

Chapter 5

1. A search of psychological journals via Proquest and PsychInfo yielded not one article of more than 300 located that was concerned with an involuntary change of name.

2. After reading Moriarty's book (2003), it is obvious that all the participants in the case were aware that "Richard" and his brother should see each other, but, as mentioned earlier, the reunion apparently never occurred.

Chapter 6

1. Initially, the program was advertised as "the ultimate reality show" (Carter, 2004), but Walters subsequently apologized for that promotion approach (Lubrano, 2004).

Chapter 7

1. There may be exceptions to this rule, depending on the state and on circumstances in a specific case.

2. Why eight months are needed by the court of appeals is unclear.

References

Adams, M. (2002). *Our son, a stranger: Adoption breakdown and its effects on parents.* Montreal: McGill-Queen's University Press.

Adoption. (1993, November 26). *CQ Researcher, 3* (44).

Adoption controversies. (1999, September 10). *CQ Researcher, 9* (34).

Adoption and Safe Families Act (1997). P. L. 105-89, 111 *Stat.*2115, 42 U.S.C. 675(5)(E).

American Academy of Pediatrics (2002a). Coparent or second-parent adoption by same-sex parents. *Pediatrics, 109,* 339-340.

American Academy of Pediatrics (2002b). Technical report: Coparent or second-parent adoption by same-sex parents. *Pediatrics, 109,* 341-344.

American Bar Association Section of Family Law (2003, August). Standards of practice for lawyers representing children in custody cases. Retrieved August 16, 2004, from www.abanet.org/family/.

American Civil Liberties Union (2004). Petition for Writ of certiorari.

American Law Institute (2002). Principles of the Law of Family Dissolution: Analysis and recommendations. Philadelphia: The Institute.

Amlung, P. K. S. (1990). Conflicts of interest in independent adoptions. *University of Cincinnati Law Review, 59,* 169-190.

Anonymous (2004a, March 31). Mother who offered twins on Internet wins in court. *The Philadelphia Inquirer,* p. A4.

Anonymous (2004b, August 3). Reduce time in foster care: Kent parental rights case ought to spur efforts to streamline appeals process. *The Grand Rapids Press.* Retrieved August 10, 2004, from www.mlive.com/news/grpress/index .ssf?/base/news-1/1091544403282220.xml.

Appell, A. R. (2003). Survey of state utilization of adoption with contact. *Adoption Quarterly, 6,* 75-86.

"Around the nation." (2004, January 29). *Chicago Daily Law Bulletin,* p. 3.

Associated Press (2004, December 31). Amid custody battle, toddler visits birth mom. Retrieved December 31, 2004, via Lexis-Nexis.com.

Associated Press (2005a, January 10). Justices reject gay adoption appeal. Retrieved January 10, 2005, from MSNBC.com.

Associated Press (2005b, February 6). Child abuse suspects held in Utah. *The New York Times,* p. 14.

Associated Press (2006, February 23). Pair say not guilty to caging children. *The Philadelphia Inquirer,* p. A12.

When Adoptions Go Wrong
© 2006 by The Haworth Press, Inc. All rights reserved.
doi:10.1300/5780_10

Associated Press Online (2003, August 2). Baby Jessica marks 10 years with family. Retrieved July 31, 2004, via Lexis-Nexis.com.

Ball, C. A. & Pea, J. A. (1998). Warring with Wardle: Morality, social science, and gay and lesbian parents. *U. of Illinois Law Review,* 253-339.

Barth, R. P. & Berry, M. (1988). *Adoption and disruption: Rates, risks, and responses.* New York: Aldine de Gruyter.

Barth, R. P. & Brooks, D. (1997). A longitudinal study of family structure and size and adoption outcomes. *Adoption Quarterly, 1* (1), 29-56.

Barth, R. P. & Miller, J. M. (2000). Building effective post-adoption services: What is the empirical foundation? *Family Relations, 49,* 447-455.

Barton, J. (2003, April 24). Appellate court strikes down "invasive" adoption law. Associated Press State and Local Wire. Retrieved July 31, 2004, from Lexis-Nexis.com.

Bebensee, P. K. (1993). In the best interests of children and adoptive parents: The need for disclosure. *Iowa Law Review, 78,* 397-426.

Beck, M. (2002). Toward a national putative father registry database. *Harvard Journal of Law and Public Policy, 25,* 1031-1080.

Bergquist, K. J. S., Campbell, M. E., & Unrau, Y. A. (2003). Caucasian parents and Korean adoptees: A survey of parents' perceptions. *Adoption Quarterly, 6* (4), 41-58.

Berry, M. (1993). Risks and benefits of open adoption. *The Future of Children, 3* (1), 125-138.

Binstock, A. T. (2004). Not if, but when?: Dismantling the Florida Adoption Act of 2001. *Cardozo Women's Law Journal, 10,* 625-657.

Blair, J. A. (1993). Gregory K. and emerging children's rights. *Trial, 29* (6), 22-26.

Bonina, D. I. & Bahe-Jachna, R. A. (1999, Spring). Human rights: The treatment of children as chattel in recent adoption decisions. *Human Rights Magazine.* Retrieved January 8, 2005, from www.abanet.org/irr/hr/sp99bonina.html.

Boone, J. L., Hostetter, M. K., & Weitzman, C. C. (2003). The predictive accuracy of pre-adoptive video review in adoptees from Russian and Eastern European orphanages. *Clinical Pediatrics, 42,* 585-590.

Bowman, B. B. (1995). Children's perspectives of disrupted adoptions: A qualitative study of lives within the child welfare system. Doctoral dissertation, University of Oregon.

Boyer, B. A. & Lubet, S. (2000). The kidnapping of Edgardo Mortara: Contemporary lessons in the child welfare wars. *Villanova Law Review, 45,* 245-288.

Bozzomo, J. W. & Scolieri, G. (2004). A survey of unified family courts: An assessment of different jurisdictional models. *Family Court Review, 42,* 12-38.

Brice, J. (2005, January 7). Judge: Evan must be with birth mother. *First Coast News.* Retrieved January 8, 2005, from Firstcoastnews.com.

Brodzinsky, D. M. (2003, October 29). Adoption by lesbians and gays: A national survey of adoption agency policies, practices, and attitudes. New York: Evan B.

Donaldson Adoption Institute. Retrieved July 29, 2004, from http://www
.adoptioninstitute.org/whowc/Gay%20and%20Lesbian%20adoption1.html.

Brodzinsky, D. M., Smith, D. W., & Brodzinsky, A. B. (1998). Children's adjustment to adoption: Developmental and clinical issues. *Developmental Clinical
Psychology and Psychiatry, 38*. Thousand Oaks, CA: Sage.

Bryant, T. (2004, March 31). High Court overturns adoption of Internet twins/
Judges reject stripping of parental rights. *St. Louis Post-Dispatch*, p. A1.

Burr v. Board of County Commissioners, 23, Ohio St. 3d 69, 391 N.E.2d 1101
(1986).

Carter, B. (2004, April 28). "The ultimate reality show" on adoption. *The New York
Times*, pp. Arts 1, 8.

Cohen, T. (2003). Note: Protecting or dismantling the family: A look at foster families and homosexual parents after *Lofton v. Kearny. Temple Political and Civil
Rights Law Review, 13*, 227-251.

Connolly, C. (1998). The description of gay and lesbian families in second-parent
adoption cases. *Behavioral Sciences and the Law, 16*, 225-236.

Connolly, C. (2002). The voice of the petitioner: The experiences of gay and lesbian
parents in successful second-parent adoption proceedings. *Law and Society Review, 36*, 325-347.

Cooper, A. M. (2004). Student note: Gay and lesbian families in the 21st century:
What makes a family? Addressing the issue of gay and lesbian adoption. *Family
Court Review, 42*, 178-192.

Cooper-Hilbert, B. (1998). *Infertility and involuntary childlessness*. New York:
W. W. Norton.

Crouch, J. (2003, Fall). New standards for child representation in custody cases.
AFCC Newsletter, 22 (4), pp. 6-7.

Cunningham, L. (2002, March 4). Gay-adoption ban goes to court. *Broward Daily
Business Review, 44* (58), A1.

Curtis, C. M. & Denby, R. W. (2004). Impact of the Adoption and Safe Families Act
(1997) on families of color: Workers share their thoughts. *Families in Society,
85*, 71-79.

Daniluk, J. C. & Hurtig-Mitchell, J. (2003). Themes of hope and healing: Infertile
couples' experiences of adoption. *Journal of Counseling and Development, 81*,
389-399.

Day, P. (2000). Rights of children: Should children be able to divorce their parents?
Journal of Contemporary Legal Issues, 11, 652-655.

DeBoer v Schmidt, 442 Mich 648 (1993a).

DeBoer v. Schmidt, 114 S.Ct. 11 (1993b).

Denniston, L. (1995, February 14). Justices delay in giving adopted boy to father.
The Philadelphia Inquirer, p. A3.

Developments in the Law: VI. Unified family courts and the child protection dilemma. (2003). *Harvard Law Review, 116*, 2099-2122. Retrieved July 28, 2004
from Lexis-Nexis Academic.

Dolgin, J. L. (1997). The fate of childhood: Legal models of children and the parent-child relationship. *Albany Law Journal, 61,* 345-431.

Donnelly, B. W. & Voydanoff, P. (1991). Factors associated with releasing for adoption among adolescent mothers. *Family Relations, 40,* 404-410.

Durcan, J. & Appell, A. R. (2001). Minor birth mothers and consent to adoption: An anomaly in youth law. *Adoption Quarterly, 5* (1), 69-79.

DuRocher, R. (1994). Balancing competing interests in post-placement adoption custody disputes: How do the scales of justice weigh the rights of biological parents, adoptive parents, and children? *The Journal of Legal Medicine, 15,* 305-343.

Dwyer, J. G. (2003). A taxonomy of children's existing rights in state decision making about their relationships. *William and Mary Bill of Rights Journal, 11,* 845-990.

Dyer, F. J. (1999). *Psychological consultation in parental rights cases.* New York: Guilford Press.

Eisen, C. R. (1998). Using a "brief case plan" method to reconcile kinship rights and the best interests of the child when an unwed father contests a mother's decision to place an infant for adoption. *Nova Law Review, 23,* 339-404.

Elrod, L. D. (1996). *Child custody practice and procedure.* Deerfield, IL: Clark, Boardman, Callaghan.

Erikson, E. H. (1950). *Childhood and society.* New York: W. W. Norton.

Evan B. Donaldson Adoption Institute (2000, March). *Adoption in the United States: A fact sheet update.* Retrieved from http://www.adoptioninstitute.org/tml.

Festinger, T. (1986). *Necessary risk: A study of adoptions and disrupted adoptive placements.* Washington, DC: Child Welfare League of America.

Festinger, T. (2002). After adoption: Dissolution or permanence? *Child Welfare, 81,* 515-533.

Festinger, T. & Pratt, R. (2002). Speeding adoptions: An evaluation of the effects of judicial continuity. *Social Work Research, 26,* 217-224.

Fleisher, A. (2003). The decline of domestic adoption: Intercountry adoption as a response to local adoption laws and proposals to foster domestic adoption. *Southern California Review of Law and Women's Studies, 13,* 171-197.

France, D. (2004, November 22). Hell house revisited. *New York,* pp. 40-45, 125.

Freundlich, M. & Peterson, L. (1998). *Wrongful adoption: Law, policy, and practice.* Washington: CWLA Press.

Freundlich, M. & Peterson, L. (1999, May). Wrongful adoption: Litigation/practice issues. Ithaca, NY: New York State Citizens Coalition for Children, Inc. Retrieved August 1, 2004, from www.nysccc.org/wrongfuladopt/litigatnotes.htm.

Gesing, E. (2004). The fight to be a parent: How courts have restricted the constitutionally-based challenges available to homosexuals. *New England Law Review, 38,* 841-896.

Gibbs v. Ernst, 538 Pa. 193, 647 A.2d 882 (1994).

Glazer, S. (1993, November 26). Outlook: Uniform law proposed. *The CQ Researcher, 3*, 1051-1052.

Goldstein, J. & Goldstein, S. (1996). "Put yourself in the skin of the child," she said. *Psychoanalytic Study of the Child, 51*, 46-55.

Gomes, C. (2003). Partners as parents: Challenges faced by gays denied marriage. *The Humanist, 63* (6), 14-19.

Goodenough v. Mass. Department of Public Health. 440 Mass. 309, 798 NE2d 941 (2003).

Graham, K. A. (2006, February 11). You took my childhood. *The Philadelphia Inquirer,* pp. A1, A6.

Graham, K. A. & Shiffman, J. (2004, July 13). Starvation case couple enter pleas. *The Philadelphia Inquirer,* pp. A1, A8.

Grahm, K. A. & Shiffman, J. (2006, February 9). Starved son set to face mother. *The Philadelphia Inquirer,* p. B4.

Graham, T. (2005a, January 19). Starvation case down to one party. *The Philadelphia Inquirer,* p. B4.

Graham, T. (2005b, November 11). Mother's plea ends starvation case in N.J. *The Philadelphia Inquirer,* pp. A1, A14.

Graham, T. (2005c, November 17). $12.5 million settlement OKd in starvation case. *The Philadelphia Inquirer,* p. B12.

Greenhouse, L. (2005, January 11). Justices refuse to consider law banning gay adoption. *The New York Times,* A14.

Greiner, K. (2004). Foster care and adoption. *Georgetown Journal of Gender and the Law, 5*, 503-528.

Groza, V., Maschmeier, C., Jamison, C., & Piccola, T. (2003). Siblings and out-of-home placements: Best practices. *Families in Society, 84*, 480-490.

Groza, V., Ryan. S. C., & Cash, S. J. (2003). Institutionalization, behavior and international adoption: Predictors of behavior problems. *Journal of Immigrant Health, 5*, 5-17.

Hansen, M. (1996, March). High court rejects Baby Emily appeal. *A. B. A. Journal, 82*, 40.

Harding, T. B. (2001). Involuntary termination of parental rights: Reform is needed. *Brandeis Law Journal, 39*, 895-921.

Haugaard, J. J., West, N. M., & Moed, A. M. (2000). Research digest: Open adoptions: Attitudes and experiences. *Adoption Quarterly, 4* (2), 89-99.

Heldman, J. K. (2003). Court delay and the waiting child. *San Diego Law Review, 40*, 1001-1038.

Henderson, S. (2005, January 11). Justices let stand Florida's law that prevents gay adoptions. *The Philadelphia Inquirer,* p. A4.

Hevesi, D. (1992, October 28). Court denies father's late request to overturn adoption. *The New York Times,* p. B6.

Hoge, W. (2001, April 10). British judge sends infants adopted on web back to St. Louis. *The New York Times,* p. A3.

Hollinger, J. H. (1995). Adoption and aspiration: The Uniform Adoption Act, the DeBoer-Schmidt case, and the American quest for the ideal family. *Duke Journal of Gender Law and Policy, 2,* 15- 40.

Hollingsworth, L. D. (2003). When an adoption disrupts: A study of public attitudes. *Family Relations, 52,* 161-166.

Holt, M. I. (2001). *Indian orphanages.* Lawrence, KS: University Press of Kansas.

Hong, K. E. (2003). Parens patriarchy: Adoption, eugenics, and same-sex couples. *California Western Law Review, 40,* 1-77.

Hughes, D. A. (1999). Adopting children with attachment problems. *Child Welfare, 78,* 541-560.

Hwang, S. L. (2004, September 29). "Open adoptions" easing placement of U.S. children. Retrieved October 6, 2004, from www.dailystar.com/dailystar/ printDS/ 41077.php.

In re the Petition of Doe, 627 N.E. 2d (Ill.App.Ct.1993).

In re Petition of Doe, 638 N.E. 2d 181, 182, (Ill. 1994).

Jeanine B. v. McCallum. No. 93-C-0547, U. S. District Court, Eastern District of Wisconsin. Retrieved May 21, 2004, from http://www.childrensrights.org/ Legal/JeanineThompson.html.

Johnson, S. M. & O'Connor, E. (2002). *The gay baby boom: The psychology of gay parenthood.* New York: New York University Press.

Judge, S. (2003). Determinants of parental stress in families adopting children from Eastern Europe. *Family Relations, 52,* 241-248.

Karst, K. L. (2003). Law, cultural conflict, and the socialization of children. *California Law Review, 91,* 967-1028.

Katz, K. D. (2004). Survey of New York law: Family law. *Syracuse Law Review, 54,* 1127-1178.

Kay, J. W. (2002, April 10). Family Solo wonders: Are we saving the children? Who do our children's protection laws really protect? *Western Massachusetts Law Tribune (Family Law), 3* (8), p. 10.

Kenyon, G. L., Chong, K-A., Erikoff-Sage, M., Hill, C., Mays, C., & Rochelle, L. (2003). Public adoption by gay and lesbian parents in North Carolina: Policy and practice. *Families in Society, 84,* 571-575.

Kim, C. (2003). Recent court decisions impacting juveniles: Case spotlight: *Lofton v. Kearney* 157 F. Supp. 2d 1372 (S.D.Fla. 2001). *UC Davis Journal of Juvenile Law and Policy, 7,* 400-408.

Kirby, K. M. & Hardesty, P. H. (1998). Evaluating older pre-adoptive foster children *Professional Psychology, 29,* 428-436.

Kirkland, K. (2003). A legal perspective on family psychology and family law: Comment on the special issue. *Journal of Family Psychology, 17,* 263-266.

Kolata, G. (2004, May 11). The heart's desire. *The New York Times,* pp. F1, F6.

Kopels, S. (1995).Wrongful adoption: Litigation and liability. *Families in Society, 76,* 20-29.

Kreeger, J. L. (2003). Family psychology and family law—a family court judge's perspective: Comment on the special issue. *Journal of Family Psychology, 17,* 260-262.

Krementz, J. (1993). *How it feels to be adopted.* New York: Knopf.

KSDK NewsChannel 5 (2004, July 9). Judge removes himself from "Internet Twins" case. Retrieved March 6, 2006.

Ladner, J. A. (2000, September). Children in out-of-home placements. *Children's Roundtable #4.* Washington, DC: The Brookings Institution. Retrieved May 21, 2004, from http://www.brookings.ed/comm/childrensrountable/issue4.htm.

Landsman, M. J., Thompson, K., & Barber, G. (2003). Using mediation to achieve permanency for children and families. *Families in Society, 84,* 229-239.

Lawrence v. Texas, 123 S. Ct. 2472 (2003).

Lifton, B. J. (1988). *Lost and found: The adoption experience.* New York: Perennial Library.

Lifton, B. J. (1994). *Journey of the adopted self: A quest for wholeness.* New York: Basic Books.

Lipka, M., Shiffman, J., & Graham, K. (2004, October 10). N. J. starvation-case brothers thriving. *The Philadelphia Inquirer,* B1, B5.

Lofton v. Kearney, 157 F.Supp.2d 1372 (S.D.Fla. 2001).

Lowe, A. D. (1996). Parents and strangers: The Uniform Adoption Act revisits the parental rights doctrine. *Family Law Quarterly, 30,* 379-425.

Lowery, C. R. (1984). The wisdom of Solomon: Criteria for child custody from the legal and clinical points of view. *Law and Human Behavior, 8,* 371-380.

Lubet, S. (1999). Book review: Judicial kidnapping, then and now: The case of Edgardo Mortara. *Northwestern University Law Review, 93,* 961-975.

Lubrano, A. (2004, April 29). Walters apologizes for "20/20" adoption ads. *The Philadelphia Inquirer,* pp. E1, E7.

Mannis, V. S. (2000). The adopting single mother: Four portraits of American women adopting from China. *Adoption Quarterly, 4* (2), 29-55.

Marian Adoption Services (1999, September 29). Discover the adoption dimension in clinical practice: A symposium for mental health professionals. Lafayette Hill, PA.

Markowitz, D. L. (2005). *The Vermont guide to civil unions.* Monpelier, VT: Office of the Secretary of State. Retrieved March 8, 2006.

Mason, M. A. (1994). *From father's property to children's rights: The history of child custody in the United States.* New York: Columbia University Press.

McBride, J. (2004, August 28). Four to share visitation of 2-year-old child. *Amarillo Globe-News.* Retrieved January 4, 2005.

McDonald, T. P., Propp, J. R., & Murphy, K. C. (2001). The postadoption experience: Child, parent, and family predictors of family adjustment to adoption. *Child Welfare, 80* (1), 71-93.

McKenna, C. L. (2004). To unknown male: Notice of plan for adoption in the Florida 2001 Adoption Act. *Notre Dame Law Review, 79,* 789-813.

McQuillan, J., Greil, A. J., White, L., & Jacob, M. C. (2003). Frustrated fertility: Infertility and psychological distress among women. *Journal of Marriage and Family, 65,* 1007-1018.

Melina, L. R. & Roszia, S. K. (1993). *The open adoption experience: A complete guide for adoptive and birth families—from making the decision through the child's growing years.* New York: Harper Perennial.

Meyer, D. D. (1999). Family ties: Solving the constitutional dilemma of the faultless father. *Arizona Law Review, 41,* 753- 846.

Mississippi Band of Choctaw Indians v. Holyfield, 490 U.S.30 (1988).

Morgan, L. W. (1998). Telling the truth in adoption proceedings: Tort actions for wrongful adoption. *Divorce Litigation, 10* (1), 11-18.

Moriarty, K. (2003). *Baby Richard—A four-year-old comes home.* Gainesville, FL: Open Door Publishing, Inc.

Mullin, E. S., & Johnson, L. (1999). The role of birth/previously adopted children in families choosing to adopt children with special needs. *Child Welfare, 78,* 579-591.

Mulvihill, G. (2005). Lawyers for starved boys haven't responded to $10 million settlement offer. *Associated Press State and Local Wire.* Retrieved April 17, 2005, from Lexis-Nexis.com.

National Adoption Information Clearinghouse (2003a, February). Openness in adoption: A bulletin for professionals. Retrieved July 29, 2004, from http://www.nccanch.acf.hhs.gov.

National Adoption Information Clearinghouse (2003b, October). Retrieved July 29, 2004, from http://nccanch.acf.hhs.gov.

NBC News Transcripts (2004a, June 3). Retrieved January 1, 2006, from http://web.lexisnexis.com.

NBC News Transcripts (2004b, December 31). Retrieved January 1, 2005, from Lexis-Nexis.com.

Nicholson, L. A. (2002). Adoption medicine and the internationally adopted child. *American Journal of Law and Medicine, 28,* 473-490.

Nordgren, S. (1997, January 21). Father of disputed child leaves. *The Philadelphia Inquirer,* p. A3.

O'Connell v. Kirchner, 115 S.Ct. 1084 (February 13, 1995).

Olsen, T. G. (1995, September/October). Bob Greene's Richard file. *Columbia Journalism Review* (unpaged).

Parness, J. A. (2003). Participation of unwed biological fathers in newborn adoptions: Achieving substantive and procedural fairness. *Journal of Law and Family Studies, 5,* 223-237.

Pertman, A. (2000). *Adoption nation: How the adoption revolution is transforming America.* New York: Basic Books.

Pertman, A. (2003, October 29). Adoption by gays and lesbians: New study shows most agencies now accept homosexuals as parents. New York: Evan B. Donaldson

Adoption Institute. Retrieved August 11, 2004, from www.try.org/newsletter/GayLesbStudy.html.

Portwood, S. G. & Repucci, N. D. (1994). Intervention versus interference: The role of the courts in child placement. In J. Blacher (Ed.), *When there's no place like home: Options for children living apart from their natural families* (pp. 3-35). Baltimore: Paul H. Brookes.

Reding, A. M. (2003). *Lofton v. Kearney:* Equal protection mandates equal rights. *U. C. Davis Law Review, 36,* 1285-1312.

Reitz, M. & Watson, K. W. (1992). *Adoption and the family system: Strategies for treatment.* New York: Guilford.

Resnik, S. A. (1996). Seeking the wisdom of Solomon: Defining the rights of unwed fathers in newborn adoptions. *Seton Hall Legislative Journal, 20,* 363-431.

Rodham, H. (1979). Children's rights: A legal perspective. In P. A. Vardin & I. N. Brody (Eds.), *Children's rights: Contemporary perspectives* (pp. 21-36). New York: Teachers College Press.

Rosenberg, E. B. (1992). *The adoption life cycle: The children and their families through the years.* New York: The Free Press.

Rosenberg, S. K. (1998). *Adoption and the Jewish family: Contemporary Perspectives.* Philadelphia: Jewish Publication Society.

Rosenman, A. S. (1995). Babies Jessica, Richard, and Emily: The need for legislative reform of adoption laws. *Chicago-Kent Law Review, 70,* 1851-1895.

Rosettenstein, D. S. (1995). Trans-racial adoption in the United States and the impact of considerations relating to minority population groups on international adoptions in the United States. *International Journal of Law and the Family, 9,* 131-154.

Ross, C. J. (2004). The tyranny of time: Vulnerable children, "bad" mothers, and statutory deadlines in parental termination proceedings. *Virginia Journal of Social Policy and the Law, 11,* 176-228.

Russ, G. H. (1993). Through the eyes of a child, "Gregory K.": A child's right to be heard. *Family Law Quarterly, 27,* 365-394.

Salter, J. (2004, May 24). Judge delays decision in case of Internet twins. *Associated Press.* Retrieved July 11, 2004, from Lexis-Nexis Academic.

Scarnecchia, S. (1994). Who is Jessica's mother? Defining motherhood through reality. *American University Journal of Gender and the Law, 3,* 1-13.

Scarnecchia, S. (1995). A child's right to protection from transfer trauma in a contested adoption case. *2, Duke Journal of Gender Law and Policy,* 41-61.

Schwartz, L. L. (1983). Contested adoption cases: Grounds for conflict between psychology and the law. *Professional Psychology, 14,* 444-456.

Schwartz, L. L. (1986). Unwed fathers and adoption custody disputes. *American Journal of Family Therapy, 14,* 347-355.

Schwartz, L. L. (1988). Surrogate motherhood II: Reflections after "Baby M." *American Journal of Family Therapy, 16,* 158-166.

Schwartz, L. L. (1991). *Alternatives to infertility: Is surrogacy the answer?* New York: Brunner/Mazel.

Schwartz, L. L. (1993a). The interaction of field theory, family systems theory, and children's rights. *American Journal of Family Therapy, 21,* 267-273.

Schwartz, L. L. (1993b). What is a family?: A contemporary view. *Contemporary Family Therapy, 15,* 429-442.

Schwartz, L. L. (1994). The challenge of raising one's non-biological children. *American Journal of Family Therapy, 22,* 195-207.

Schwartz, L. L. (2000a). Adoption: Parents who choose their children and their options. In F. W. Kaslow (Ed.), *Handbook of couples and family forensics* (pp. 23-42). New York: John Wiley.

Schwartz, L. L. (2000b). Families by choice: Adoptive and foster families. In W. C. Nichols, M. A. Pace-Nichols, D. S. Beevar, & A. Y. Napier (Eds.), *Handbook of family development* (pp. 255-278). New York: John Wiley.

Schwartz, L. L. (2003). A nightmare for King Solomon: The new reproductive technologies. *Journal of Family Psychology, 17,* 229-237.

Schwartz, L. L. & Isser, N. K. (2000). *Endangered children: Neonaticide, infanticide, and filicide.* Boca Raton, FL: CRC Press.

Schwartz, L. L. & Kaslow, F. W. (2003). *Welcome home! An international and nontraditional adoption reader.* Binghamton, NY: The Haworth Press.

Shapiro, V. B., Shapiro, J. R., & Paret, I. H. (2001a). *Complex adoption and assisted reproductive technology: A developmental approach to clinical practice.* New York: Guilford.

Shapiro, V. B., Shapiro, J. R, & Paret, I. H. (2001b). International adoption and the formation of new family attachment. *Smith College Studies in Social Work, 71,* 389-420.

Sheeran, T. J. (2006, February 22). Adullt kids testify in caged children case. *Dayton Daily News.* Retrieved February 23, 2006, from www.daytondailynews.com.

Sherman, W. & Port, B. (2004, May 22). Judge gives custody of identical twins to casino dad. *New York Daily News.* Retrieved July 16, 2004, from Lexis-Nexis Academia.

Shiffman, J. (2004, September 21). Records reviewed in starvation case. *The Philadelphia Inquirer,* p. B3.

Shiffman, J., Lipka, M., & Graham, K. A. (2004, May 6). Parents of gaunt N. J. sons indicted. *The Philadelphia Inquirer,* pp. A1, A6.

Shireman, J. F. (1995). Adoption by single parents. *Marriage and Family Review, 20,* 367-388.

Siegel, D. H. (2003). Open adoption of infants: Adoptive parents' feelings seven years later. *Social Work, 48,* 409-419.

Spofford, B. Z. (1993). Antecedents of American adoption. *The Future of Children, 3* (1), 17-25.

State Bar of Michigan. (2001, February). Adoption in the media. *Michigan Bar Journal, 80,* 29.

Steinberg, N. (2002, September 19). Anatomy of Bob Greene. Retrieved August 7, 2004, from www.salon.com/news/feature/2002/09/19/greene/print.html.

Storck, D. (1981, July 14). Infant victims of real problem. *The Philadelphia Inquirer,* p. B1.

Strasser, M. (2004). Adoption and the best interests of the child: On the use and abuse of studies. *New England Law Journal, 38,* 629-642.

Tasker, F. L. & Golombok, S. (1997). *Growing up in a lesbian family.* New York: Guilford Press.

Tenenbaum, J. D. (1996). Introducing the Uniform Adoption Act. *Family Law Quarterly, 30,* 333-343.

Testa, M. F. (2004). When children cannot return home: Adoption and guardianship. *The Future of Children, 14* (1), 115-129.

Trethan, P. (2004, April 29). Book review: How life changes after upward-bound teen becomes pregnant. *The Philadelphia Inquirer,* p. E2.

Tunstall, J. (2005, September 14). Dollars plead no contest, get 15 years in prison. *Tampa Tribune.* Retrieved February 9, 2006, from TBO.com.

Tye, M. C. (2003). Lesbian, gay, bisexual, and transgender parents: Special considerations for the cutody and adoption evaluator. *Family Court Review, 41,* 92-103.

Uniform Adoption Act., 9 U. L. A. Part 1 (West Supp., 1995).

Vansickle, A. & Krueger, C. (2005, February 5). Citrus couple arrested, face abuse charges. *Citrus Times,* p.1. Retrieved February 5, 2005, from Lexis-Nexis .com.

Vonk, M. E. (2001). Cultural competence for transracial adoptive parents. *Social Welfare, 46,* 246-255.

Vonk, M. E., Simms, P. J., & Nackerud, L. (1999). Political and personal aspects of intercountry adoption of Chinese children in the United States. *Families in Society, 80,* 496-505.

Wainright, J. L., Russell, S. T., & Patterson, C. J. (2004). Psychosocial adjustment, school outcomes, and romantic relationships of adolescents with same-sex parents. *Child Development, 75,* 1886-1898.

Wambaugh, C. L. (1999). Biology is important, but does not necessarily always constitute a "family": A brief survey of the Uniform Adoption Act. *Akron Law Review, 32,* 791-832.

Ward, M. (1997). Family paradigms and older-child adoption: A proposal for matching parents' strengths to children's needs. *Family Relations, 46,* 257-252.

Ward v. Ward, 742 So.2d 250 (Fla. Dist. Ct. App. 1996).

Wardle, L. D. (1997). The potential impact of homosexual parenting on children. *University of Illinois Law Review,* 833-920.

Wardle, L. D. (2004). Adult sexuality, the best interests of children, and placement liability of foster-care and adoption agencies. *Journal of Law and Family Studies, 6,* 59-99.

Weaver-Catalana, B. (1995). The battle for Baby Jessica: A conflict of best interests. *Buffalo Law Review, 43*, 583-615.

Weiner, I. B. & Elkind, D. (1978). *Child development: A core approach.* New York: John Wiley.

White, S. R. (1997a). "Baby Richard FAQ—1 of 3: Current events. Retrieved August 7, 2004, from www.webcom.com/kmc/adoption/br-faq-1.html.

White, S. R . (1997b). "Baby Richard" FAQ—2 of 3: The transfer. Retrieved August 7, 2004, from www.webcom.com/kmc/adoption/br-faq-2.html.

White, S. R. (1997c). "Baby Richard" FAQ—3 of 3: Background. Retrieved August 7, 2004, from www.webcom.com/kmc/adoption/br-faq-3.html.

Wilson, B. (2004a, September 10). Judge rules for biological mother. *Amarillo Globe-News.* Retrieved from www.amarillonet.com/stories/091004/new_judge rule.shtml.

Wilson, B. (2004b, September 21). Girl to return to birth mom immediately. Retrieved from www.amarillonet.com/stories/092104/new_girlto.shtml.

Winkler, R. C., Brown, D. W., van Keppel, M., & Blanchard, A. (1988). *Clinical practice in adoption.* New York: Pergamon Press.

Word, R. (2005, January 16). Woman hands over boy she raised. *The Philadelphia Inquirer,* p. A13.

Worden, A. (2004, June 5). Pa. adoption law limits time birth parents can reconsider. *The Philadelphia Inquirer,* pp. A1, A6.

Wu, C. N. (2002). Making families and children a high priority in the courts: California's center for families, children and the courts. *Family Court Review, 40,* 417-434.

Zinman, D. C. (1992). Father knows best: The unwed father's right to raise his infant surrendered for adoption. *Fordham Law Review, 60,* 971-1001.

Index

Page numbers followed by the letter "f" indicate a figure; those followed by the letter "e" indicate exhibits.

When Adoptions Go Bad
© 2006 by The Haworth Press, Inc. All rights reserved.
doi:10.1300/5780_11

Order a copy of this book with this form or online at:
http://www.haworthpress.com/store/product.asp?sku=5780

WHEN ADOPTIONS GO WRONG
Psychological and Legal Issues of Adoption Disruption

_____ in hardbound at $24.95 (ISBN-13: 978-0-7890-3181-5; ISBN-10: 0-7890-3181-7)

_____ in softbound at $14.95 (ISBN-13: 978-0-7890-3182-2; ISBN-10: 0-7890-3182-5)

124 pages plus index

Or order online and use special offer code HEC25 in the shopping cart.

COST OF BOOKS_____

☐ **BILL ME LATER:** (Bill-me option is good on US/Canada/Mexico orders only; not good to jobbers, wholesalers, or subscription agencies.)

☐ Check here if billing address is different from shipping address and attach purchase order and billing address information.

POSTAGE & HANDLING_____
(US: $4.00 for first book & $1.50 for each additional book)
(Outside US: $5.00 for first book & $2.00 for each additional book)

Signature_____

SUBTOTAL_____

☐ **PAYMENT ENCLOSED: $_____**

IN CANADA: ADD 7% GST_____

☐ **PLEASE CHARGE TO MY CREDIT CARD.**

STATE TAX_____
(NJ, NY, OH, MN, CA, IL, IN, PA, & SD residents, add appropriate local sales tax)

☐ Visa ☐ MasterCard ☐ AmEx ☐ Discover
☐ Diner's Club ☐ Eurocard ☐ JCB

Account # _____

FINAL TOTAL_____
(If paying in Canadian funds, convert using the current exchange rate, UNESCO coupons welcome)

Exp. Date_____

Signature_____

Prices in US dollars and subject to change without notice.

NAME_____

INSTITUTION_____

ADDRESS_____

CITY_____

STATE/ZIP_____

COUNTRY_____ COUNTY (NY residents only)_____

TEL_____ FAX_____

E-MAIL_____

May we use your e-mail address for confirmations and other types of information? ☐ Yes ☐ No
We appreciate receiving your e-mail address and fax number. Haworth would like to e-mail or fax special discount offers to you, as a preferred customer. **We will never share, rent, or exchange your e-mail address or fax number.** We regard such actions as an invasion of your privacy.

Order From Your Local Bookstore or Directly From
The Haworth Press, Inc.
10 Alice Street, Binghamton, New York 13904-1580 • USA
TELEPHONE: 1-800-HAWORTH (1-800-429-6784) / Outside US/Canada: (607) 722-5857
FAX: 1-800-895-0582 / Outside US/Canada: (607) 771-0012
E-mail to: orders@haworthpress.com

For orders outside US and Canada, you may wish to order through your local sales representative, distributor, or bookseller.
For information, see http://haworthpress.com/distributors

(Discounts are available for individual orders in US and Canada only, not booksellers/distributors.)
PLEASE PHOTOCOPY THIS FORM FOR YOUR PERSONAL USE.
http://www.HaworthPress.com   BOF06